SKILL SHARPENERS
Math 2

◀ Keep Your Child's Academic Skills Sharp

This book belongs to

name

Editorial Development: Vicky Shiotsu
Content Editing: Kathleen Jorgensen
Copy Editing: Laurie Westrich
Art Direction: Yuki Meyer
Illustration: Mary Rojas
Design/Production: Jessica Onken

EMC 8252

Visit
teaching-standards.com
to view a correlation
of this book.
This is a free service.

**Correlated to
Current Standards**

**Congratulations on your purchase of some of the
finest teaching materials in the world.**

Evan-Moor Corporation
phone 1-800-777-4362, fax 1-800-777-4332.
Entire contents © 2020 Evan-Moor Corporation
18 Lower Ragsdale Drive, Monterey, CA 93940-5746. Printed in China.

CPSIA: Asia Pacific Offset Ltd, Kowloon, Hong Kong [1/2022]

Dear student,

Math is all around us. If you want to know "**how much**," "**how many**," "**how tall**," "**what time**," or "**what shape**," you need math! This fun workbook will help you practice.

Many pages show you objects to help you add and subtract. You can use real objects, too!

There are lots of ways to solve problems. Some are shown in an example on the page. Study the example and try it, or use your favorite strategy.

Some of the problems are word problems that tell a little story. Put yourself in the story to solve them.

If you <u>get stuck</u>, ask yourself these questions:

⭐ What is the goal of the problem?

⭐ What information do I have already?

⭐ What do these numbers have to do with each other?

⭐ Should I add or subtract?

⭐ Do I need to figure out another number before I can find the answer?

When you finish this workbook, your skills will be **super sharp!**

super sharp!

Sincerely,

Your friends at Evan-Moor

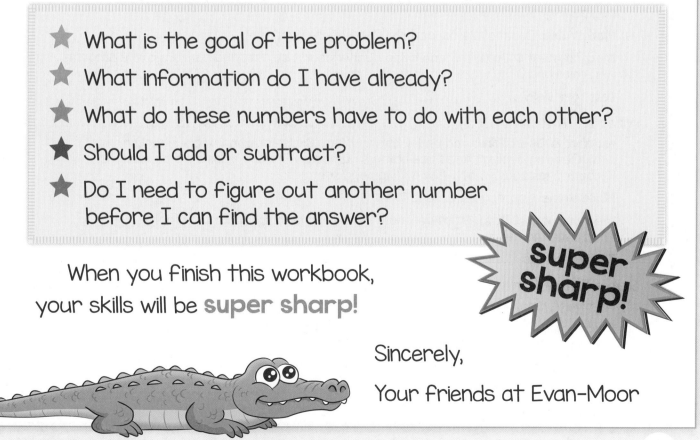

Contents

Ready, Set, Relay!

Solve the problems to help the animals finish their relay.

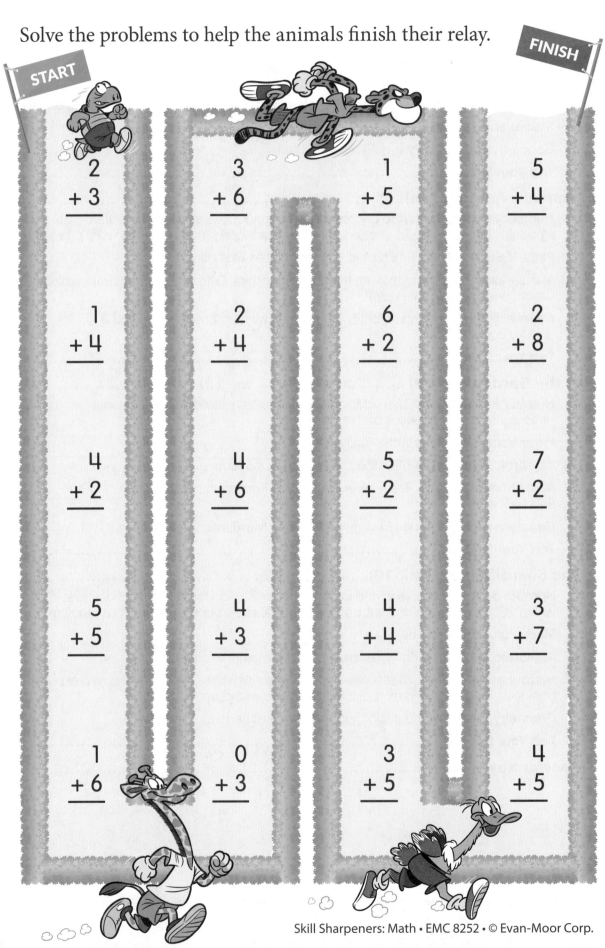

START

FINISH

$$2 \atop +3$$ $$3 \atop +6$$ $$1 \atop +5$$ $$5 \atop +4$$

$$1 \atop +4$$ $$2 \atop +4$$ $$6 \atop +2$$ $$2 \atop +8$$

$$4 \atop +2$$ $$4 \atop +6$$ $$5 \atop +2$$ $$7 \atop +2$$

$$5 \atop +5$$ $$4 \atop +3$$ $$4 \atop +4$$ $$3 \atop +7$$

$$1 \atop +6$$ $$0 \atop +3$$ $$3 \atop +5$$ $$4 \atop +5$$

Fun and Games

6

Skill:
Subtract
within 10

Solve each problem to help Hector Hamster finish the obstacle course.

START HERE

$$\begin{array}{r} 5 \\ -3 \\ \hline \end{array}$$ $$\begin{array}{r} 6 \\ -3 \\ \hline \end{array}$$ $$\begin{array}{r} 3 \\ -2 \\ \hline \end{array}$$ $$\begin{array}{r} 9 \\ -6 \\ \hline \end{array}$$

$$\begin{array}{r} 10 \\ -1 \\ \hline \end{array}$$ $$\begin{array}{r} 9 \\ -5 \\ \hline \end{array}$$ $$\begin{array}{r} 8 \\ -4 \\ \hline \end{array}$$ $$\begin{array}{r} 7 \\ -4 \\ \hline \end{array}$$ $$\begin{array}{r} 5 \\ -4 \\ \hline \end{array}$$

$$\begin{array}{r} 4 \\ -2 \\ \hline \end{array}$$ $$\begin{array}{r} 5 \\ -5 \\ \hline \end{array}$$ $$\begin{array}{r} 7 \\ -2 \\ \hline \end{array}$$

$$\begin{array}{r} 10 \\ -5 \\ \hline \end{array}$$

$$\begin{array}{r} 8 \\ -6 \\ \hline \end{array}$$

$$\begin{array}{r} 4 \\ -3 \\ \hline \end{array}$$

$$\begin{array}{r} 6 \\ -4 \\ \hline \end{array}$$ $$\begin{array}{r} 8 \\ -2 \\ \hline \end{array}$$ $$\begin{array}{r} 10 \\ -6 \\ \hline \end{array}$$ $$\begin{array}{r} 6 \\ -2 \\ \hline \end{array}$$

$$\begin{array}{r} 8 \\ -3 \\ \hline \end{array}$$ $$\begin{array}{r} 8 \\ -5 \\ \hline \end{array}$$

$$\begin{array}{r} 5 \\ -0 \\ \hline \end{array}$$ $$\begin{array}{r} 6 \\ -6 \\ \hline \end{array}$$

$$\begin{array}{r} 5 \\ -1 \\ \hline \end{array}$$ $$\begin{array}{r} 7 \\ -3 \\ \hline \end{array}$$ $$\begin{array}{r} 9 \\ -7 \\ \hline \end{array}$$

FINISH

© Evan-Moor Corp. • EMC 8252 • *Skill Sharpeners: Math*

Fun and Games

Shot Put Contest

Five animals entered the shot put contest. Here are the scores.

Name	First Throw (meters)	Second Throw (meters)
Gogo Gorilla	6	9
Iggy Iguana	6	7
Tuffy Toad	8	9
Millie Moose	5	4
Elmer Elephant	7	8

Add the scores for the first throw and the second throw for each animal. Write the totals in the table.

Name	Total Meters Thrown
Gogo Gorilla	
Iggy Iguana	
Tuffy Toad	
Millie Moose	
Elmer Elephant	

Who had the highest total? _____

What was the total? _____

Who had the lowest total? _____

What was the total? _____

Which two animals had the same total?

_____   _____

What was their total? _____

Fun and Games

Write the sums and follow the signs. Good luck!

Skill:
Add within 20

This way →   **Sharp turn**

6	5	4	9	7	9
+ 7	+ 6	+ 7	+ 5	+ 5	+ 3

9	6	8	8	4	8
+ 6	+ 9	+ 8	+ 4	+ 8	+ 5

Hard left   ← **Back this way**

9	2	8	7	9	6
+ 9	+ 8	+ 3	+ 7	+ 7	+ 6

Last turn

7	6	9	8	6	9
+ 6	+ 5	+ 4	+ 7	+ 8	+ 8

You've made it out!

Fun and Games

Ball Toss

Each player tossed a ball two times. Write an equation to show how far the ball traveled.

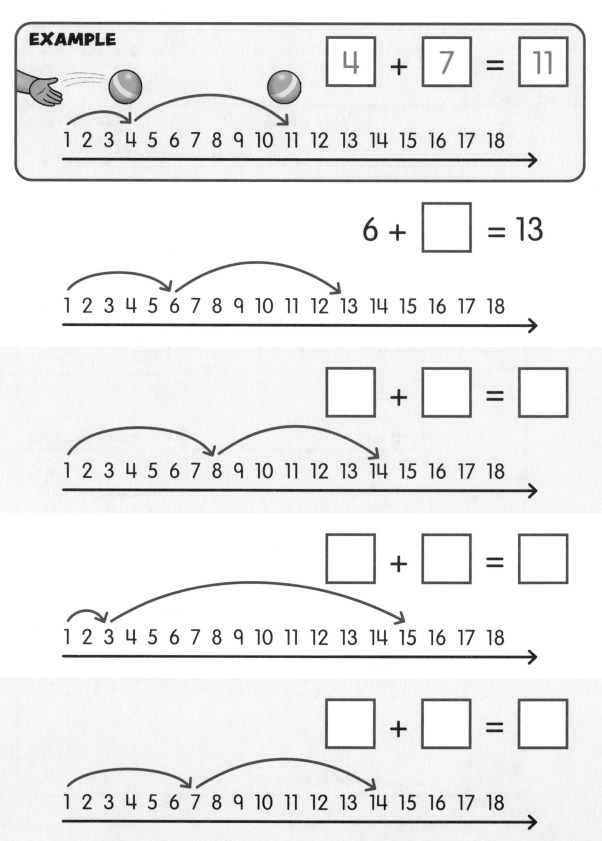

EXAMPLE

4 + 7 = 11

1 2 3 4 5 6 7 8 9 10 11 12 13 14 15 16 17 18

$6 +$ ☐ $= 13$

1 2 3 4 5 6 7 8 9 10 11 12 13 14 15 16 17 18

☐ + ☐ = ☐

1 2 3 4 5 6 7 8 9 10 11 12 13 14 15 16 17 18

☐ + ☐ = ☐

1 2 3 4 5 6 7 8 9 10 11 12 13 14 15 16 17 18

☐ + ☐ = ☐

1 2 3 4 5 6 7 8 9 10 11 12 13 14 15 16 17 18

Fun and Games

Skill:
Subtract within 20

Dudley Dog needs help to reach the finish line. First subtract. Then color all the squares with the same answer as Dudley's number.

START

12 − 7	16 − 7	13 − 5	14 − 7	17 − 8	15 − 9
13 − 8	11 − 6	14 − 9	10 − 5	13 − 9	12 − 9
14 − 5	12 − 5	16 − 9	11 − 6	12 − 7	14 − 9
18 − 9	11 − 8	13 − 7	17 − 9	16 − 8	13 − 8

FINISH

Fun and Games

Run, Run, Run!

Skills:
Read a table;
Add and subtract
within 20

Six runners ran a long race. The table shows how long it took each runner to complete the race.

Name	Time on Stopwatch
Diego Duck	15 minutes
Harriet Horse	8 minutes
Tina Tiger	12 minutes
Gerry Giraffe	7 minutes
Elmer Elephant	9 minutes
Morty Mouse	11 minutes

Who won the race? _____

How much faster was the winning time
than the slowest time? _____ minutes

Who finished 3 minutes after Elmer? _____

How many minutes faster was Harriet
than Diego? _____ minutes

How many minutes faster was Gerry
than Morty? _____ minutes

Who finished 3 minutes after Harriet? _____

Fun and Games

Solve the problems. Then color the boxes that have an answer of 9 or 14. You'll see how many races Robbie Rabbit won!

Skill:
Add and subtract within 20

9 + 9	8 + 6	7 + 6	5 + 9	14 − 7	12 − 8
8 + 5	18 − 9	15 − 7	7 + 7	16 − 8	6 + 6
8 + 8	13 − 4	15 − 6	16 − 7	17 − 8	9 + 7
17 − 9	5 + 7	7 + 8	9 + 5	16 − 9	15 − 9
18 − 8	11 − 8	15 − 8	12 − 3	6 + 5	12 − 9

Robbie won _____ races.

Fun and Games

A Poky Racer

Connect the dots from 80 to 120 to find the animal.

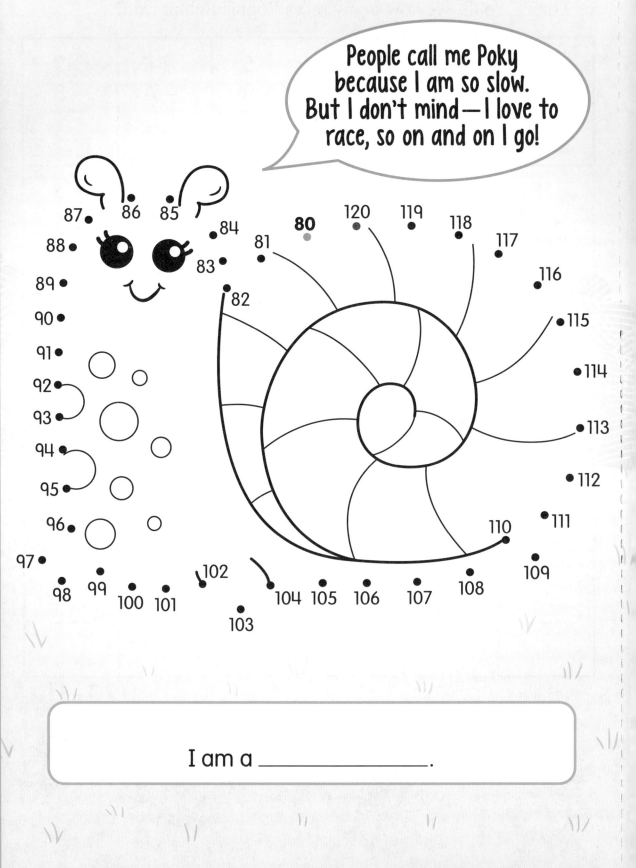

People call me Poky because I am so slow. But I don't mind—I love to race, so on and on I go!

Fun and Games

I am a _____.

Write the times for each event.

Skill:
Tell time to the half hour

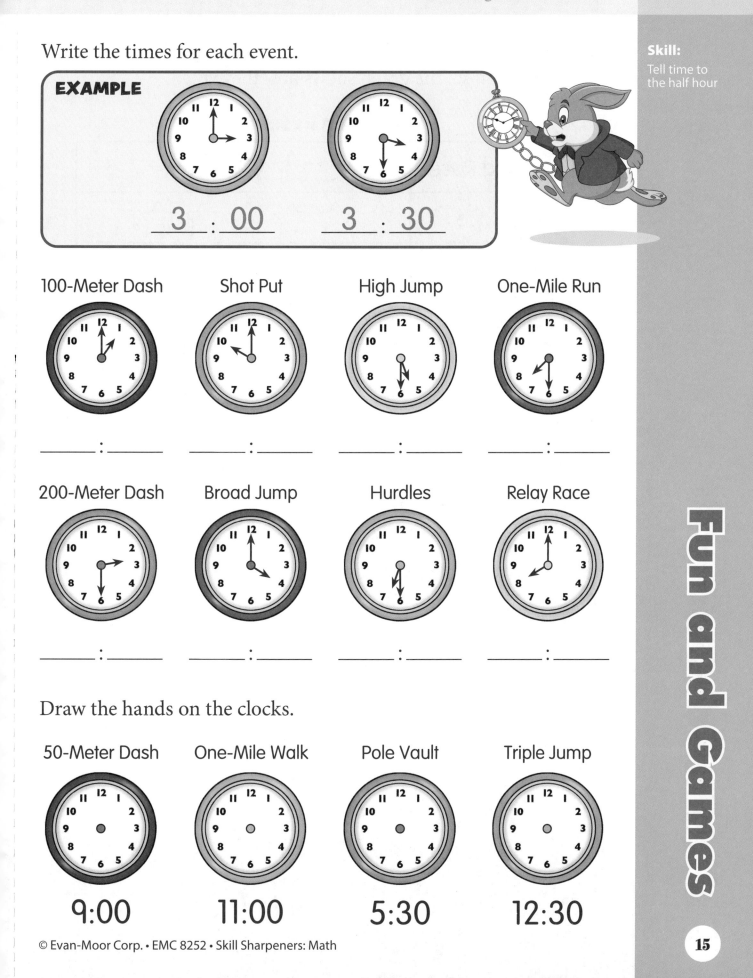

EXAMPLE

___3__ : 00   ___3__ : 30

100-Meter Dash   Shot Put   High Jump   One-Mile Run

_____ : _____   _____ : _____   _____ : _____   _____ : _____

200-Meter Dash   Broad Jump   Hurdles   Relay Race

_____ : _____   _____ : _____   _____ : _____   _____ : _____

Draw the hands on the clocks.

50-Meter Dash   One-Mile Walk   Pole Vault   Triple Jump

9:00   11:00   5:30   12:30

Fun and Games

Some animals were asked to vote for the event they enjoyed watching the most. The graph shows how they voted.

Favorite Events

Running Race	☆ ☆ ☆ ☆ ☆
Relay Race	☆ ☆ ☆ ☆ ☆ ☆
Ball Toss	☆ ☆ ☆
Obstacle Race	☆ ☆ ☆ ☆

☆ = 1 vote

Which event got the most votes? _____

How many more animals chose the
running race than the ball toss? _____

How many votes did the relay race
and ball toss get together? _____

How many more animals voted for the
running race or relay race than for the
ball toss or obstacle race? _____

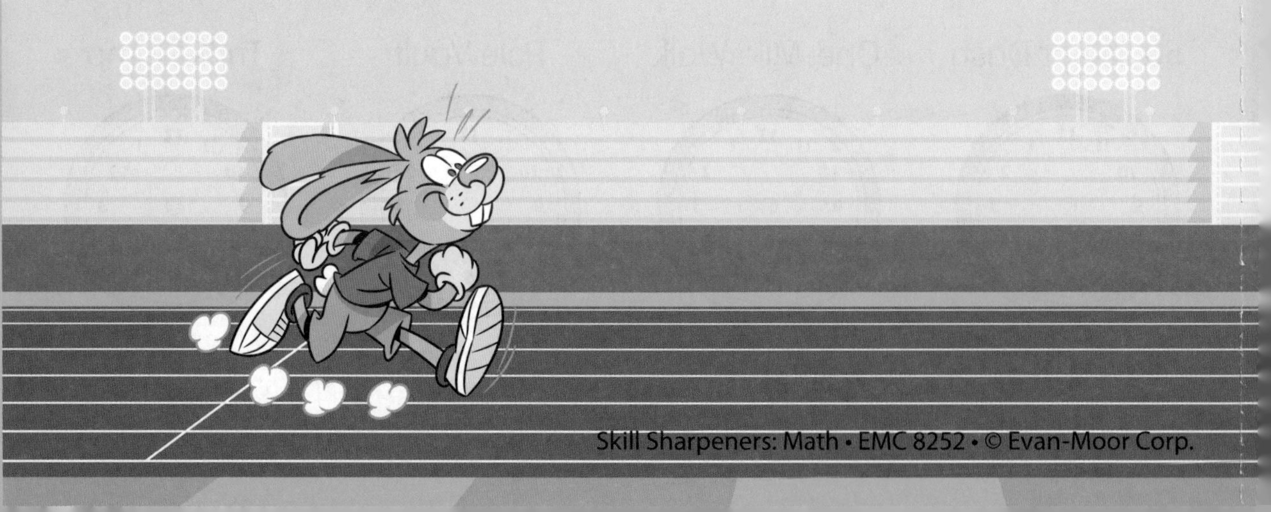

Fun and Games

Add or subtract.

6	8	5	4	7	9
+7	+9	+8	+7	+5	+7

15	12	18	14	17	13
-9	-5	-9	-6	-8	-6

Write the times.

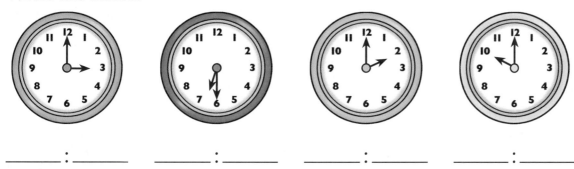

_____ : _____   _____ : _____   _____ : _____   _____ : _____

Count by 1s. Write the missing numbers on the path.

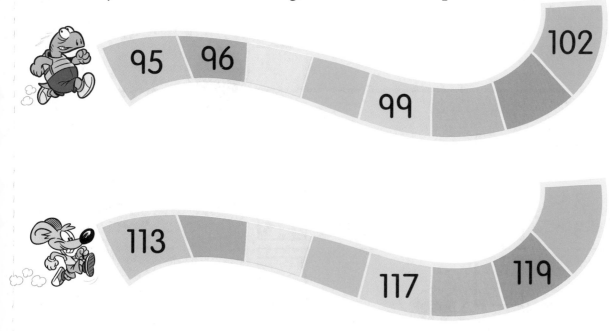

95 96 ___ ___ 99 ___ ___ 102

113 ___ ___ 117 ___ 119

Skill:
Use addition strategies (make small groups)

When you add three or more numbers, you can add pairs of numbers first.

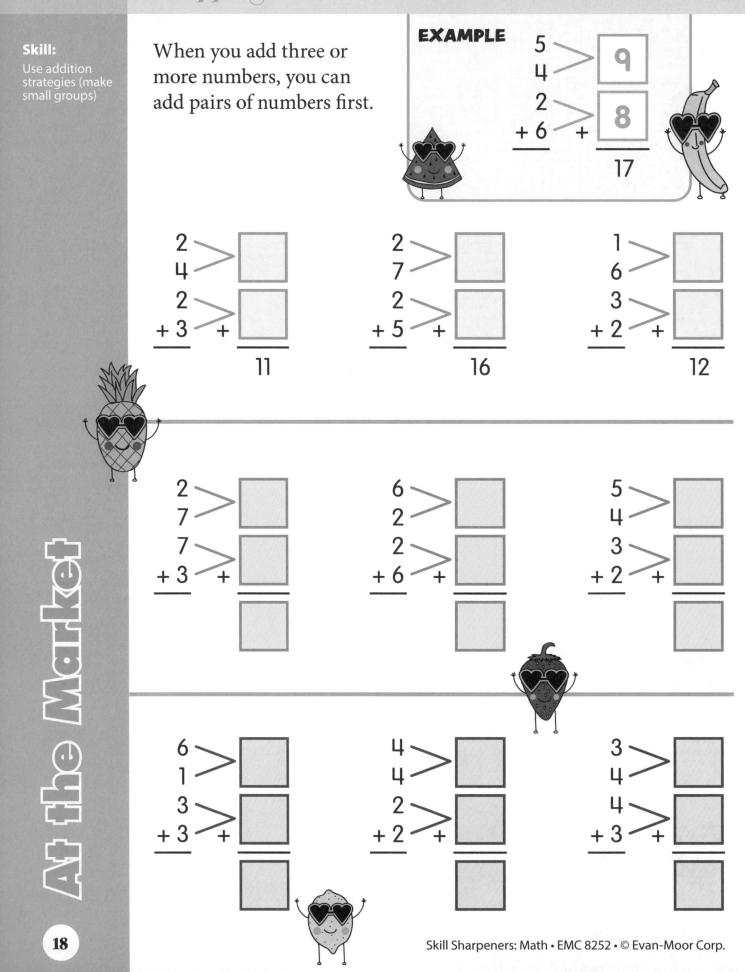

EXAMPLE

$$
\begin{array}{r}
5 \\
4
\end{array} > \boxed{9}
$$

$$
\begin{array}{r}
2 \\
+\ 6
\end{array} + \boxed{8}
$$

$$
\overline{17}
$$

At the Market

$$
\begin{array}{r}
2 \\
4
\end{array} > \square
$$
$$
\begin{array}{r}
2 \\
+\ 3
\end{array} + \square
$$
$$
\overline{11}
$$

$$
\begin{array}{r}
2 \\
7
\end{array} > \square
$$
$$
\begin{array}{r}
2 \\
+\ 5
\end{array} + \square
$$
$$
\overline{16}
$$

$$
\begin{array}{r}
1 \\
6
\end{array} > \square
$$
$$
\begin{array}{r}
3 \\
+\ 2
\end{array} + \square
$$
$$
\overline{12}
$$

$$
\begin{array}{r}
2 \\
7
\end{array} > \square
$$
$$
\begin{array}{r}
7 \\
+\ 3
\end{array} + \square
$$
$$
\square
$$

$$
\begin{array}{r}
6 \\
2
\end{array} > \square
$$
$$
\begin{array}{r}
2 \\
+\ 6
\end{array} + \square
$$
$$
\square
$$

$$
\begin{array}{r}
5 \\
4
\end{array} > \square
$$
$$
\begin{array}{r}
3 \\
+\ 2
\end{array} + \square
$$
$$
\square
$$

$$
\begin{array}{r}
6 \\
1
\end{array} > \square
$$
$$
\begin{array}{r}
3 \\
+\ 3
\end{array} + \square
$$
$$
\square
$$

$$
\begin{array}{r}
4 \\
4
\end{array} > \square
$$
$$
\begin{array}{r}
2 \\
+\ 2
\end{array} + \square
$$
$$
\square
$$

$$
\begin{array}{r}
3 \\
4
\end{array} > \square
$$
$$
\begin{array}{r}
4 \\
+\ 3
\end{array} + \square
$$
$$
\square
$$

When adding three or more numbers, you may find two numbers that add up to 10. Add those numbers first to make your adding easier. Then add the other numbers.

EXAMPLE

$$
\begin{array}{r} 5 \\ 4 \\ 2 \\ + 5 \\ \end{array}
\quad 10
\qquad
\begin{array}{r} 4 \\ + 2 \\ \end{array}
\qquad
\begin{array}{r} 10 \\ + 6 \\ \hline 16 \end{array}
$$

$$
\begin{array}{r} 4 \\ 4 \\ 6 \\ + 2 \\ \hline \end{array}
\qquad
\begin{array}{r} 4 \\ 7 \\ 2 \\ + 3 \\ \hline \end{array}
\qquad
\begin{array}{r} 4 \\ 3 \\ 2 \\ + 6 \\ \hline \end{array}
\qquad
\begin{array}{r} 4 \\ 7 \\ 5 \\ + 3 \\ \hline \end{array}
$$

$$
\begin{array}{r} 2 \\ 5 \\ 3 \\ + 5 \\ \hline \end{array}
\qquad
\begin{array}{r} 2 \\ 1 \\ 1 \\ + 8 \\ \hline \end{array}
\qquad
\begin{array}{r} 5 \\ 1 \\ 9 \\ + 2 \\ \hline \end{array}
\qquad
\begin{array}{r} 1 \\ 8 \\ 2 \\ + 7 \\ \hline \end{array}
$$

$$
\begin{array}{r} 3 \\ 1 \\ 7 \\ + 3 \\ \hline \end{array}
\qquad
\begin{array}{r} 7 \\ 7 \\ 3 \\ + 3 \\ \hline \end{array}
\qquad
\begin{array}{r} 8 \\ 6 \\ 2 \\ + 2 \\ \hline \end{array}
\qquad
\begin{array}{r} 5 \\ 3 \\ 4 \\ + 5 \\ \hline \end{array}
$$

At the Market

Skills:
Solve word
problems;
Calculate
amounts
with coins

Answer the questions.

nickel 5¢   dime 10¢   quarter 25¢

Jan wants to buy 3 pieces of candy. Each piece costs 5¢.
Jan has 2 dimes. Does she have enough money? Explain.

Yes. 5 + 5 + 5 = 15. The candy costs 15¢.
Jan has 2 dimes, which is 20¢.

Ian wants to buy a cookie. It costs 85¢. He has 7 dimes and
1 nickel. How much more money does he need?

_____

Jill has 8 nickels. Jawbreakers cost 20¢ each. How many
jawbreakers can she buy?

_____

Ryan has 2 quarters. He wants to buy a lollipop that costs 45¢.
Does he have enough money? Explain.

_____

_____

Lee has 5 dimes. She wants to buy 3 gumballs that cost 10¢
each. Does she have enough money? Explain.

_____

_____

Skill Sharpeners: Math • EMC 8252 • © Evan-Moor Corp.

At the Market

Skill:
Calculate amounts with coins and bills

How much money is in each purse?

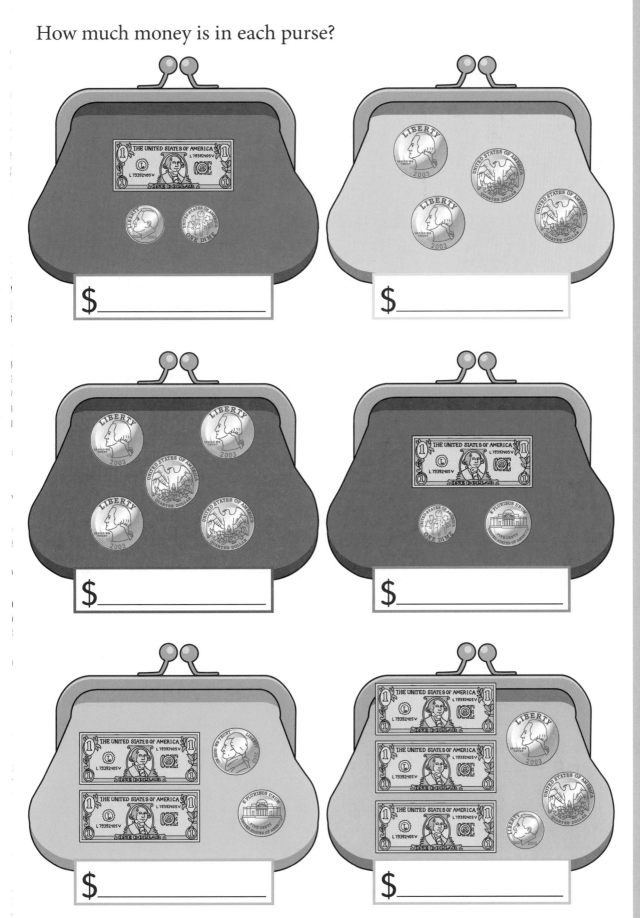

$ _____

$ _____

$ _____

$ _____

$ _____

$ _____

At the Market

Fruity Sums

You can use a doubles fact to solve a fact that is one more or one less.

$4 + 4 = 8$

$4 + 5 = 9$

$4 + 5$ is one more than $4 + 4$.

$4 + 3 = 7$

$4 + 3$ is one less than $4 + 4$.

Write the missing sums.

$3 + 3 =$ _____ $5 + 5 =$ _____ $6 + 6 =$ _____

$3 + 4 =$ _____ $5 + 6 =$ _____ $6 + 7 =$ _____

$3 + 2 =$ _____ $5 + 4 =$ _____ $6 + 5 =$ _____

$7 + 7 =$ _____ $8 + 8 =$ _____ $9 + 9 =$ _____

$7 + 8 =$ _____ $8 + 9 =$ _____ $9 + 10 =$ _____

$7 + 6 =$ _____ $8 + 7 =$ _____ $9 + 8 =$ _____

At the Market

Skill:
Identify odd and even numbers

An **even** number of things can be made into pairs with none left over. An **odd** number of things will have one left over when made into pairs.

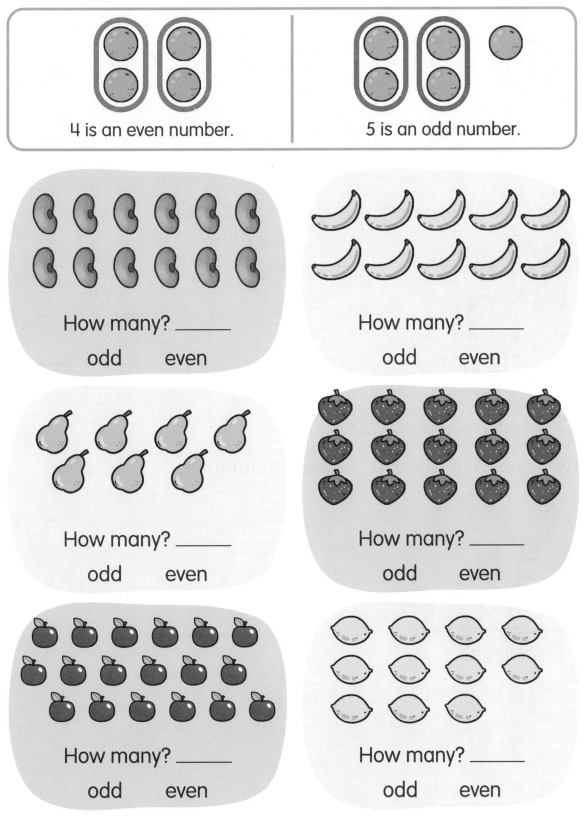

4 is an even number.	5 is an odd number.

How many? _____

odd   even

How many? _____

odd   even

How many? _____

odd   even

How many? _____

odd   even

How many? _____

odd   even

How many? _____

odd   even

At the Market

Skill:
Identify odd and
even numbers

Circle the **odd** numbers.
Draw a box around the
even numbers.

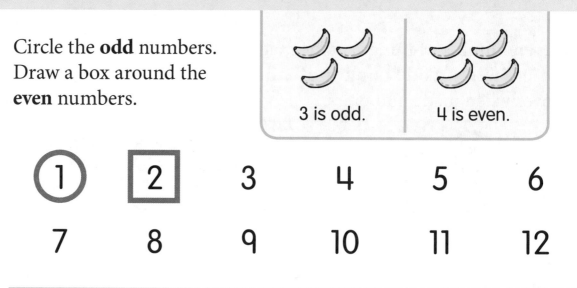

3 is odd. 4 is even.

① ☐2 3 4 5 6

7 8 9 10 11 12

Count on. Write the **even** numbers from **2** to **30**.

_____ _____ _____ _____ _____

_____ _____ _____ _____ _____

_____ _____ _____ _____ _____

Count on. Write the **odd** numbers from **1** to **29**.

_____ _____ _____ _____ _____

_____ _____ _____ _____ _____

_____ _____ _____ _____ _____

At the Market

Skill Sharpeners: Math • EMC 8252 • © Evan-Moor Corp.

Count the tens and ones. Tell how many apples.

Skill:
Compose numbers with tens and ones

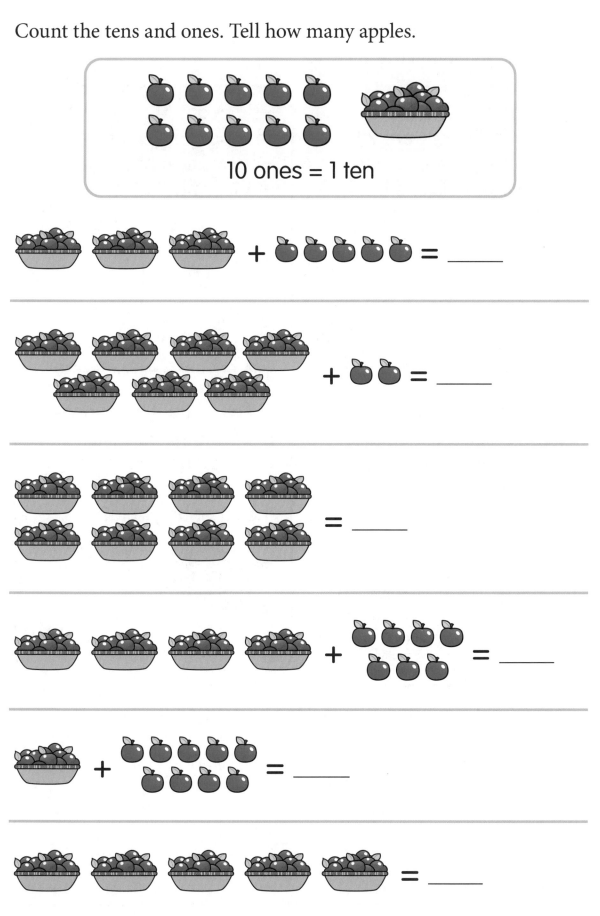

10 ones = 1 ten

+ 🍎🍎🍎🍎🍎 = _____

+ 🍎🍎🍎 = _____

= _____

+ 🍎🍎🍎🍎🍎🍎🍎 = _____

+ 🍎🍎🍎🍎🍎🍎🍎🍎🍎 = _____

= _____

At the Market

Skills:

Solve word problems; Write equations; Add and subtract within 100

Add or subtract to solve the problems.
Show how you found the answer.

Meg bought two loaves of bread. There were 24 slices in each loaf. How many slices did she buy?

$$24$$
$$+ 24$$
$$\overline{48}$$

__48__ slices

Sid bought 14 carrots. Jess bought 26 carrots. How many more carrots did Jess buy?

_____ more carrots

Kelcie bought 1 dozen eggs. She used 4 eggs to make a cake. How many eggs did Kelcie have then?

_____ eggs

Micah bought 48 ounces of beans in two bags. One bag held 16 ounces. How many ounces did the other bag hold?

_____ ounces

Jin bought two bags of nuts. One bag weighed 12 ounces. The other weighed 10 ounces more than the first bag. How much did the bags weigh in all?

_____ ounces

At the Market

Skill Sharpeners: Math • EMC 8252 • © Evan-Moor Corp.

Pete's family bought beans, peas, and corn at the market.
Find which vegetable Pete likes best. First solve the problems.
Then color the squares that have **6** in the **tens** place to see the
first letter of Pete's favorite vegetable.

Skill:
Add and subtract within 100

62 + 36	79 − 15	87 − 23	36 + 33	88 − 24
77 − 52	95 − 35	34 + 14	87 − 54	68 − 6
99 − 86	41 + 25	54 + 15	74 − 12	99 − 35
96 − 71	67 − 7	66 + 33	48 + 51	97 − 63
16 + 62	82 − 20	47 + 12	52 + 31	43 + 34
60 + 27	77 − 11	25 + 62	80 + 18	57 + 41

At the Market

Circle Pete's favorite vegetable.

The graph shows the fruits and vegetables Farmer Joe sold last Thursday. Each piece of the graph stands for one fruit or vegetable.

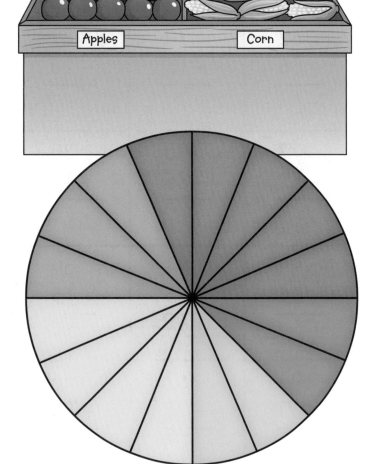

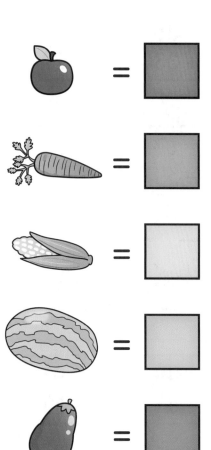

How many carrots were sold? _____

How many ears of corn were sold? _____

How many more apples were sold than eggplant? _____ more

How many fruits and vegetables were sold in all? _____

At the Market

28

There are cucumbers of all sizes at the market.
Here are some. Measure them.

Skill:
Measure length
using inches

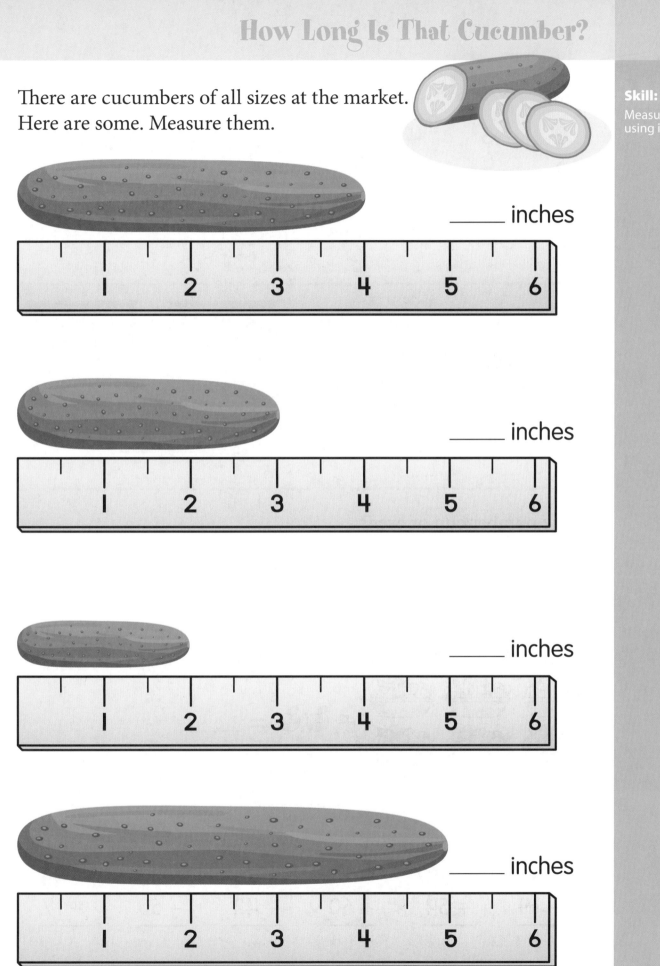

_____ inches

_____ inches

_____ inches

_____ inches

At the Market

Add.

2	3	4
5	4	8
4	5	5
+ 5	+ 2	+ 2

6 + 6 = _____   8 + 8 = _____

6 + 5 = _____   8 + 9 = _____

How much money?

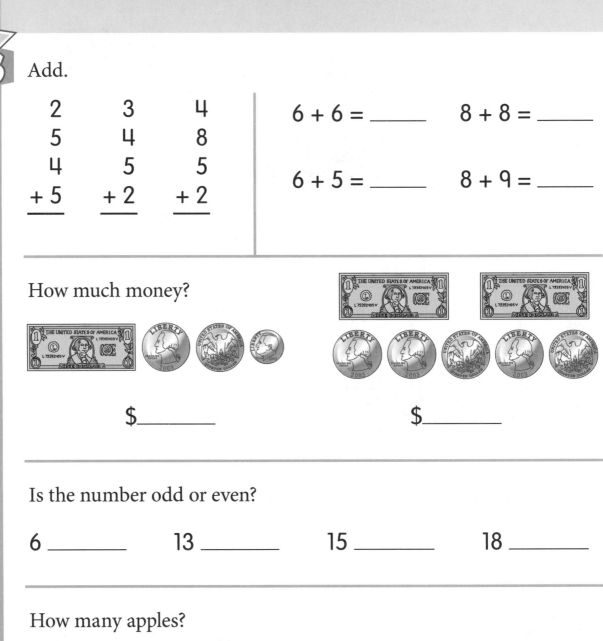

$_____ $_____

Is the number odd or even?

6 _____   13 _____   15 _____   18 _____

How many apples?

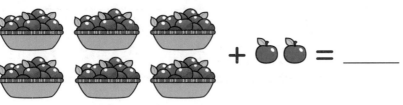

+ 🍎🍎 = _____

Add or subtract.

50	34	17	78	83	99
+ 19	+ 54	+ 60	− 42	− 60	− 17

At the Market

Add. Then find the sums that have **9** in the **ones** place. Write the letters of the problems in order on the lines to find out what's cooking!

____ ____ ____ ____

EXAMPLE

tens	ones
1	4
+ 2	3
3	7

Skill:
Add within 100

a	j	m	d	s	r	g
21 + 5	11 + 7	23 + 12	33 + 45	35 + 14	21 + 26	30 + 8

h	t	b	v	l	c	n
52 + 14	16 + 23	63 + 15	55 + 12	32 + 26	91 + 3	44 + 44

u	p	y	f	e	i	o
62 + 24	77 + 21	63 + 33	80 + 11	21 + 48	15 + 11	74 + 23

k	w	x	q	z		
34 + 32	22 + 37	64 + 20	24 + 71	42 + 35		

Surprise, Surprise!

Chef Louis has created a wonderful surprise for dessert. To find out what it is, first solve the problems. Then color each square that has an answer with **6** in the **tens** place. This will tell you the first letter of the surprise. Circle the picture of the surprise dessert.

69 − 36	79 − 15	87 − 23	96 − 33	88 − 24	47 − 11
77 − 52	95 − 35	39 − 13	87 − 54	68 − 6	90 − 60
99 − 86	87 − 25	78 − 15	74 − 12	99 − 35	72 − 41
96 − 71	67 − 7	66 − 33	68 − 55	97 − 63	88 − 64
75 − 62	82 − 20	98 − 24	99 − 4	40 − 20	56 − 25
68 − 27	77 − 11	83 − 42	96 − 40	59 − 49	58 − 12

Skill Sharpeners: Math • EMC 8252 • © Evan-Moor Corp.

In the Kitchen

Skill:

Add equal groups of numbers

Look at all the cookies that Andy baked! Circle each row. Count the number of cookies in each row. Then write an addition sentence to show how many cookies Andy made.

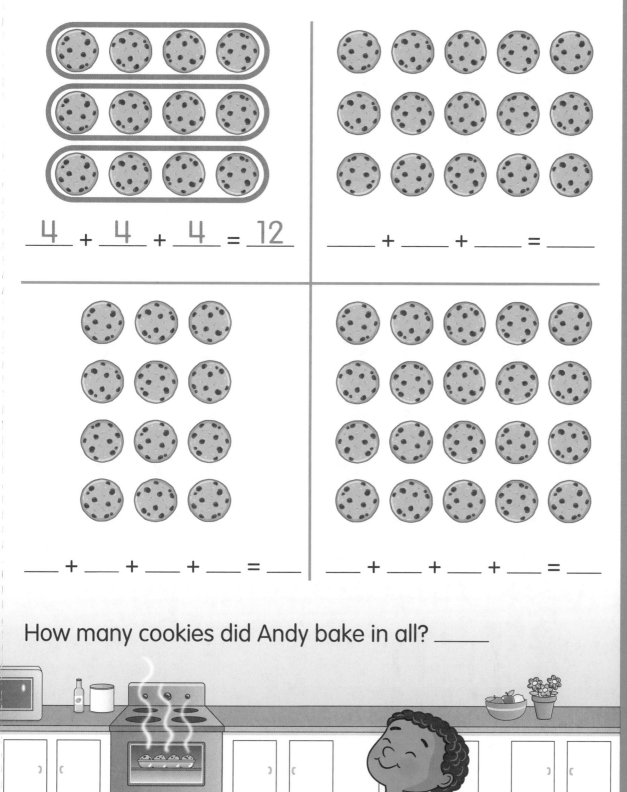

___4___ + ___4___ + ___4___ = ___12___

___ + ___ + ___ = ___

___ + ___ + ___ + ___ = ___

___ + ___ + ___ + ___ = ___

How many cookies did Andy bake in all? _____

In the Kitchen

What's in the Kitchen?

Count the number of items in each row.
Write an addition sentence to show how many there are.

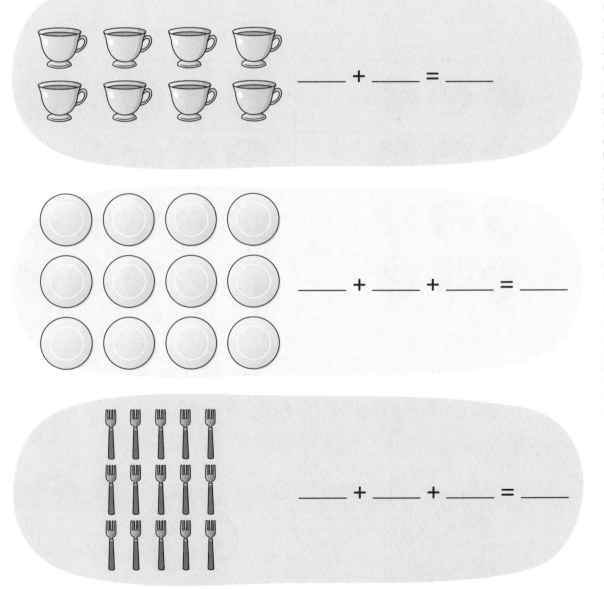

____ + ____ = ____

____ + ____ = ____

____ + ____ + ____ = ____

____ + ____ + ____ = ____

Skill Sharpeners: Math • EMC 8252 • © Evan-Moor Corp.

Cook Up Some Addition

Skill:
Use addition strategies (regrouping)

You can break up numbers to help you add.

EXAMPLE

$$45 + 26 \rightarrow \begin{array}{r} 40 + 5 \\ 20 + 6 \\ \hline 60 + 11 = 71 \end{array}$$

Show how you can break up the numbers to help you add.

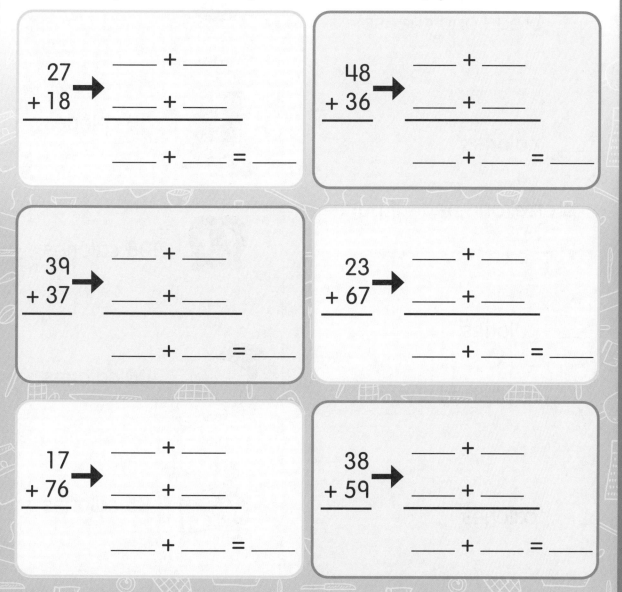

$$27 + 18 \rightarrow \begin{array}{r} \underline{} + \underline{} \\ \underline{} + \underline{} \\ \hline \underline{} + \underline{} = \underline{} \end{array}$$

$$48 + 36 \rightarrow \begin{array}{r} \underline{} + \underline{} \\ \underline{} + \underline{} \\ \hline \underline{} + \underline{} = \underline{} \end{array}$$

$$39 + 37 \rightarrow \begin{array}{r} \underline{} + \underline{} \\ \underline{} + \underline{} \\ \hline \underline{} + \underline{} = \underline{} \end{array}$$

$$23 + 67 \rightarrow \begin{array}{r} \underline{} + \underline{} \\ \underline{} + \underline{} \\ \hline \underline{} + \underline{} = \underline{} \end{array}$$

$$17 + 76 \rightarrow \begin{array}{r} \underline{} + \underline{} \\ \underline{} + \underline{} \\ \hline \underline{} + \underline{} = \underline{} \end{array}$$

$$38 + 59 \rightarrow \begin{array}{r} \underline{} + \underline{} \\ \underline{} + \underline{} \\ \hline \underline{} + \underline{} = \underline{} \end{array}$$

In the Kitchen

Skill:
Use addition
strategies
(regrouping)

Hillary is looking for a snack that has fewer than 200 calories. (A calorie is a unit of measure that tells how much energy your body gets from eating.) Here are some choices. Add to find the number of calories for each choice.

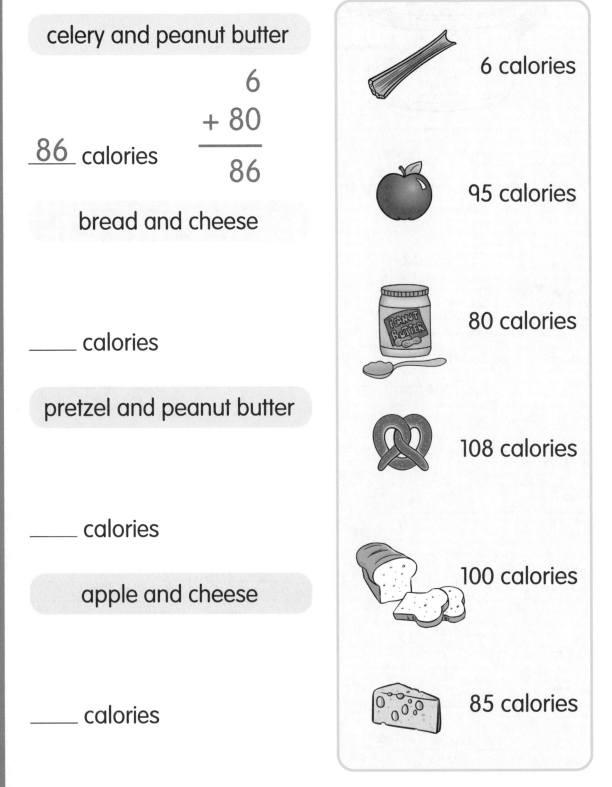

celery and peanut butter

$$
\begin{array}{r}
6 \\
+\ 80 \\
\hline
86
\end{array}
$$

__86__ calories

bread and cheese

_____ calories

pretzel and peanut butter

_____ calories

apple and cheese

_____ calories

6 calories

95 calories

80 calories

108 calories

100 calories

85 calories

In the Kitchen

Skills:
Solve word problems; Add and subtract within 100; Use addition strategies (regrouping)

Solve the problems.

Janna put 21 slices of tomatoes on a plate. Then she added 16 more slices. How many slices of tomatoes were on the plate?

_____ slices

Casey bought 2 jars of olives. He put all the olives into a bowl. There were 45 olives in each jar. How many were in the bowl?

_____ olives

Kruti made 36 sandwiches. There were 22 turkey sandwiches. The rest had tuna. How many tuna sandwiches were there?

_____ sandwiches

Jin made 48 cupcakes. There were 18 with chocolate icing. The rest had vanilla icing. How many cupcakes had vanilla icing?

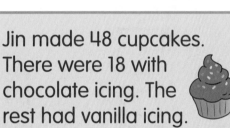

_____ cupcakes

Elina cut one cucumber into 12 slices, another into 13 slices, and another into 15 slices. How many slices did she have in all?

_____ slices

There were 64 carrot sticks. After Ryan ate some, there were 51 sticks left. How many carrot sticks did Ryan eat?

_____ carrot sticks

In the Kitchen

Skill:

Recognize relationship between addition and subtraction

Amira is doing her math homework while she waits for her meatloaf to finish cooking. Help her complete each subtraction problem. Then add to check the answers.

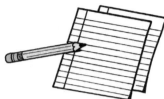

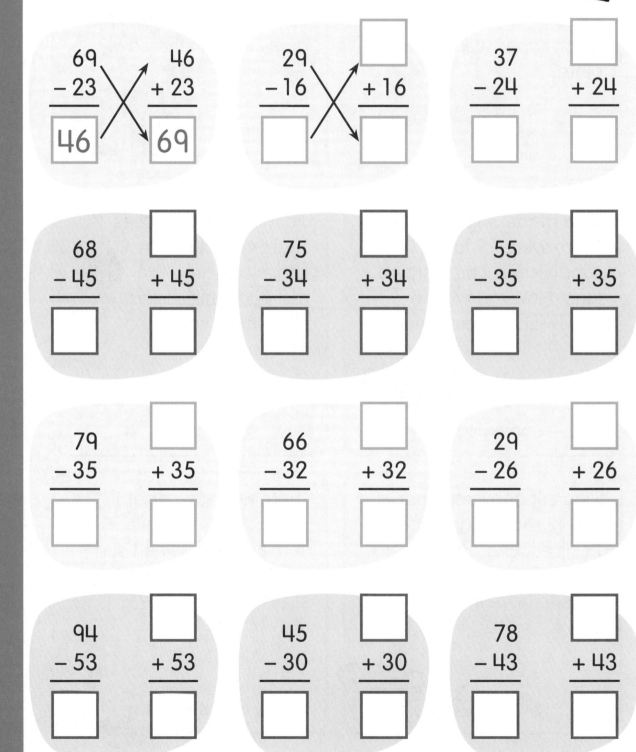

In the Kitchen

Skills:
Identify equal shares; Divide shapes into equal shares

You can slice pizza to make equal shares.

two equal shares	**three equal shares**	**four equal shares**
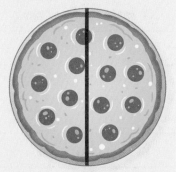	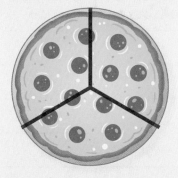	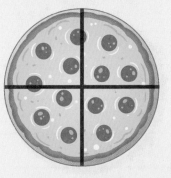
This pizza has two **halves**. Each share is called **one half**.	This pizza has three **thirds**. Each share is called **one third**.	This pizza has four **fourths**. Each share is called **one fourth**.

Write what share of pizza has been eaten.

_____   _____   _____

Slice the pizza to show equal shares. Draw toppings on the pizza to match the share.

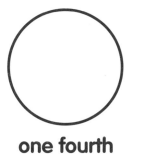      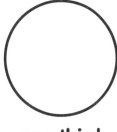

one fourth   **one half**   **one third**

In the Kitchen

Family Favorites

Skills:
Read a table;
Create a bar
graph

Alexa did a survey to see which foods the people in her family liked. She made a table to show the results.

	pizza	hamburger	taco	stir fry	hot dog
Mom	X			X	
Dad	X	X	X		X
Cleo	X	X			
Malcolm	X	X	X	X	X
Alexa	X		X	X	

Use the table to complete this graph.

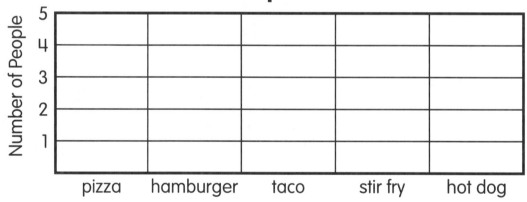

Which food did everyone like? _____

Which food did the least number of people like? _____

Which three foods got the same number of votes?

_____ _____ _____

How many votes did each of these foods get? _____

In the Kitchen

Add or subtract. Fill in the circle to show the answer.

35
+ 24
[   ]
○ 69
○ 59
○ 49

21
+ 49
[   ]
○ 60
○ 610
○ 70

67
+ 25
[   ]
○ 82
○ 92
○ 812

69
− 36
[   ]
○ 34
○ 33
○ 95

47
− 23
[   ]
○ 24
○ 80
○ 69

64
− 51
[   ]
○ 18
○ 15
○ 13

Write an addition sentence to show
how many strawberries there are.

_____ + _____ + _____ = _____

Solve.

Madi made 24 raisin
cookies and 18 oatmeal
cookies. How many
cookies did she make
in all?

_____ cookies

Draw a line to match.

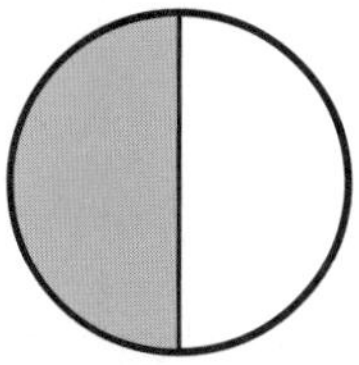

one third

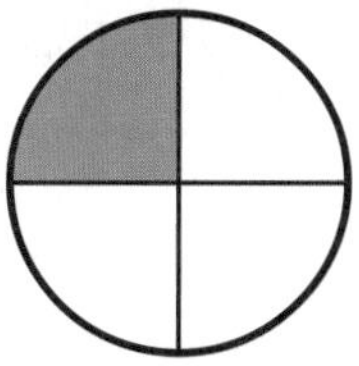

one half

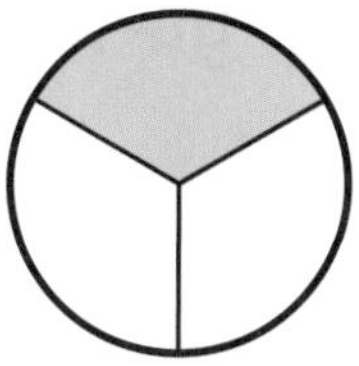

one fourth

In the Kitchen

Which Ride?

Skill:
Count by 2s,
5s, and 10s

Lizzie, Sam, and Priya followed
different paths at the amusement park.

> Lizzie took the Counting by Tens path.
> Sam took the Counting by Fives path.
> Priya took the Counting by Twos path.

Color Lizzie's path orange. Color Sam's path **blue**.
Color Priya's path green. Write each child's name
beside the ride where he or she went.

Priya

Sam

Lizzie

2	9	11	25	5	10	18	10	7	23
4	6	8	27	29	15	19	20	9	29
21	25	10	30	25	20	21	30	11	30
23	27	12	14	30	35	40	40	13	120
22	20	18	16	31	32	45	50	17	110
24	33	13	33	60	55	50	60	18	100
29	3	17	3	65	13	25	70	80	90

bumper cars

Ferris wheel

merry-go-round

_____

Amusement Park

Carla is playing "Cross the River." She must cross a river full of hungry crocodiles by jumping from rock to rock.

First Carla must solve the problems on the rocks.
Those with **even-numbered** answers are rocks she can jump on.
Those with **odd-numbered** answers are really crocodiles!

> Even numbers end in 0, 2, 4, 6, and 8.
> Odd numbers end in 1, 3, 5, 7, and 9.

Help Carla by writing the answers to the problems. Then color the rocks with even answers to make a safe path for her.

$14 - 6 = 8$

$15 - 7 =$

$12 - 8 =$

$6 + 7 =$

$8 + 8 =$

$10 - 6 =$

$18 - 9 =$

$16 - 8 =$

$7 + 5 =$

$9 + 7 =$

$8 + 7 =$

$14 - 8 =$

$5 + 7 =$

$7 + 6 =$

Amusement Park

Skills:
Add and subtract within 20;
Identify odd and even numbers

43

Funtime Buys

Theo is in the gift shop at Funtime Park.
Here are some items he is thinking of buying.
Circle the money he will need.

Skill:
Add three or more numbers within 100

Brett and Tiana took turns shooting three arrows at the target. They played three rounds. Each time, they added their points to see who got the higher score. Read the clues to find out where the arrows landed.

10
20
30
40

Round 1

Brett got a score of 60. His arrows landed on three different numbers. What were the numbers?

_____ _____ _____

Tiana got a score of 70. Her arrows landed on three different numbers. What were the numbers?

_____ _____ _____

Round 2

Brett got a score of 90. All three arrows landed on the same number. What was the number?

_____

Tiana got a score of 90, too. All three arrows landed on different numbers. What were the numbers?

_____ _____ _____

Round 3

Brett got a score of 100. One arrow landed on 30. Where did the other arrows land?

_____ _____

Tiana got a score of 100, too. One arrow landed on 20. Where did the other arrows land?

_____ _____

Amusement Park

Super-Duper Scoops

Add the numbers on the ice cream scoops. Add the ones first. Then add the tens. Add the two sums to get the total sum. Write the sum on the ice cream cone.

Add the ones.
$2 + 6 + 3 = $ **11**

Add the tens.
$10 + 10 + 20 = $ **40**

Add the two sums.
$11 + 40 = $ **51**

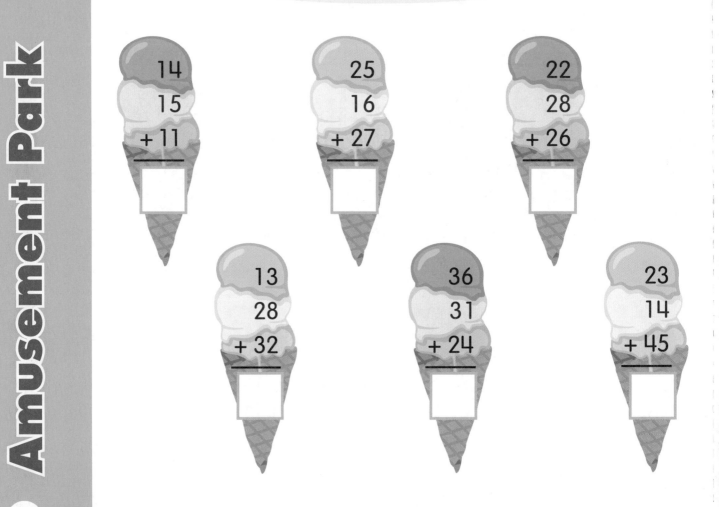

Skill Sharpeners: Math • EMC 8252 • © Evan-Moor Corp.

Skill:
Decompose
numbers

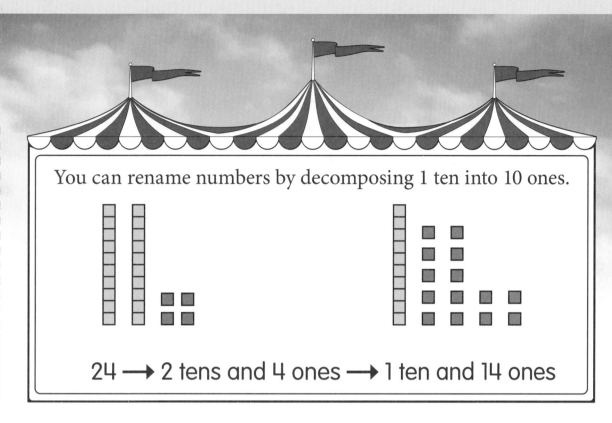

You can rename numbers by decomposing 1 ten into 10 ones.

24 ➝ 2 tens and 4 ones ➝ 1 ten and 14 ones

Show two different ways you can name each number.

27	2 tens ____ ones	1 ten ____ ones
35	3 tens ____ ones	2 tens ____ ones
41	4 tens ____ ones	3 tens ____ ones
83	8 tens ____ ones	7 tens ____ ones
62	____ tens 2 ones	____ tens 12 ones
59	____ tens 9 ones	____ tens 19 ones
74	____ tens 4 ones	____ tens 14 ones
96	____ tens 6 ones	____ tens 16 ones

Amusement Park

Tiki's Tickets

TICKETS

Skill:
Calculate amounts with coins and bills

Tiki is buying 4 ride tickets. The total cost is $4.60. Tiki has a whole pocket full of dollar bills, quarters, dimes, and nickels. Draw three ways Tiki can pay for her ride tickets. In one way, use only coins.

Way 1

Way 2

Way 3

Amusement Park

Skill Sharpeners: Math • EMC 8252 • © Evan-Moor Corp.

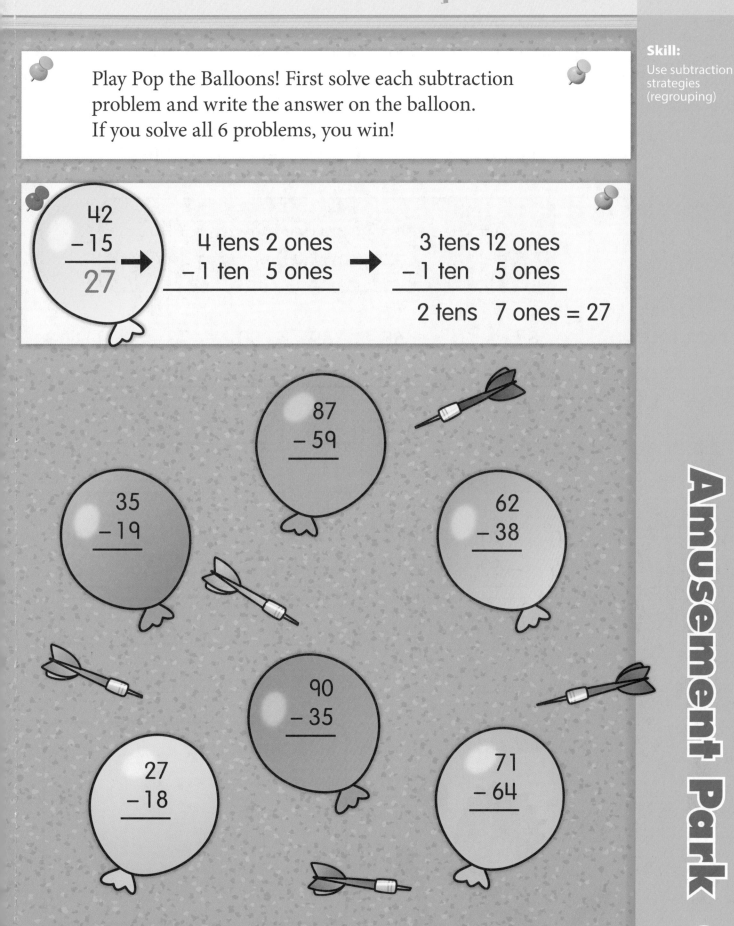

Play Pop the Balloons! First solve each subtraction problem and write the answer on the balloon.
If you solve all 6 problems, you win!

Skill:
Use subtraction strategies (regrouping)

42
−15
27
→
4 tens 2 ones
−1 ten 5 ones
→
3 tens 12 ones
−1 ten 5 ones
2 tens 7 ones = 27

87
− 59

35
−19

62
− 38

90
− 35

27
−18

71
− 64

Amusement Park

Skills:
Subtract
within 100;
Use subtraction
strategies
(regrouping)

Juggling Jim loves to tell jokes and riddles. Use the code to solve his riddle below. Write the matching letter below each answer. Then draw the answer in the box.

> **What can you wear that everyone will like?**

A – 24	E – 22	G – 53	R – 45
B – 35	I – 12	N – 16	T – 17

$$87 - 63 = \boxed{}$$
$$68 - 15 = \boxed{}$$
$$89 - 44 = \boxed{}$$
$$50 - 28 = \boxed{}$$
$$73 - 49 = \boxed{}$$
$$71 - 54 = \boxed{}$$

___   ___   ___   ___   ___   ___

$$60 - 25 = \boxed{}$$
$$74 - 62 = \boxed{}$$
$$99 - 46 = \boxed{}$$
$$82 - 29 = \boxed{}$$
$$93 - 48 = \boxed{}$$
$$48 - 36 = \boxed{}$$
$$99 - 83 = \boxed{}$$

___   ___   ___   ___   ___   ___   ___

Skill:
Use addition and subtraction strategies (regrouping)

Add or subtract.

40 − 6	72 + 9	51 − 5	32 − 4
82 − 5	48 + 5	65 − 9	33 − 7
20 − 3	90 − 1	37 + 4	74 − 8
50 − 2	22 − 4	76 + 7	63 − 9
46 − 8	55 + 9	89 + 3	62 + 8

Amusement Park

Ball Toss

Some children played Ball Toss at the amusement park. Read about how they did. Then solve the problems.

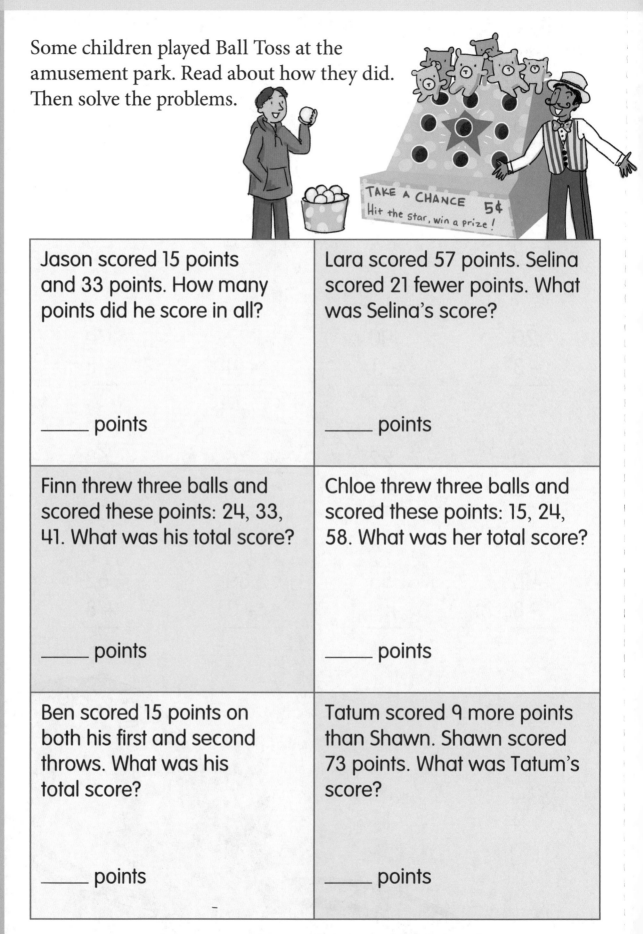

Jason scored 15 points and 33 points. How many points did he score in all? _____ points	Lara scored 57 points. Selina scored 21 fewer points. What was Selina's score? _____ points
Finn threw three balls and scored these points: 24, 33, 41. What was his total score? _____ points	Chloe threw three balls and scored these points: 15, 24, 58. What was her total score? _____ points
Ben scored 15 points on both his first and second throws. What was his total score? _____ points	Tatum scored 9 more points than Shawn. Shawn scored 73 points. What was Tatum's score? _____ points

Amusement Park

Skill:

Tell time to the quarter hour

When the minute hand is on the 9, it is 45 minutes past the hour.

8:45

When the minute hand is on the 3, it is 15 minutes past the hour.

7:15

Write the time shown on each clock.

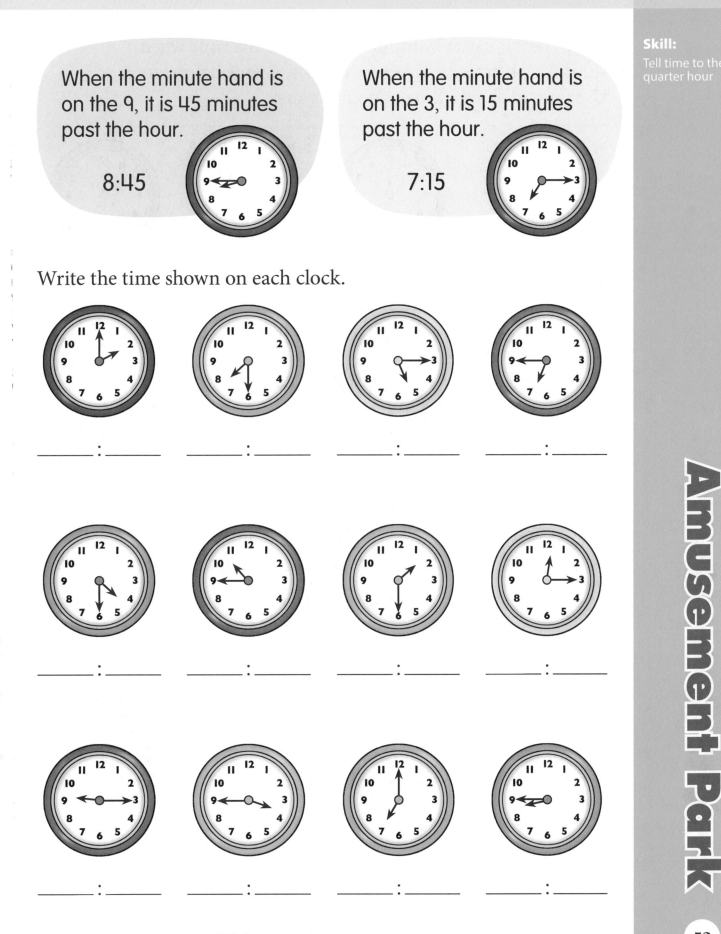

____:____   ____:____   ____:____   ____:____

____:____   ____:____   ____:____   ____:____

____:____   ____:____   ____:____   ____:____

Amusement Park

Skills:

Tell time to
the quarter
hour; Use a.m.
and p.m.

Katie spent a day at Funtime Park. Write the time when
she did each activity. Use **a.m.** to show a time before noon.
Use **p.m.** to show a time of noon or later.

Katie and her
family arrived
at the park in
the morning.

10:00 a.m.

She rode the
Ferris wheel
right after
she arrived.

_____

She went on the
roller coaster
before lunch.

_____

Katie and
her family
had lunch.

_____

After lunch, she
played Ring Toss
and won!

_____

After Ring Toss,
she went on
a boat ride.

_____

Katie had ice
cream for an
afternoon
snack.

_____

Katie and her
family went
home before
dinner.

_____

Add or subtract.

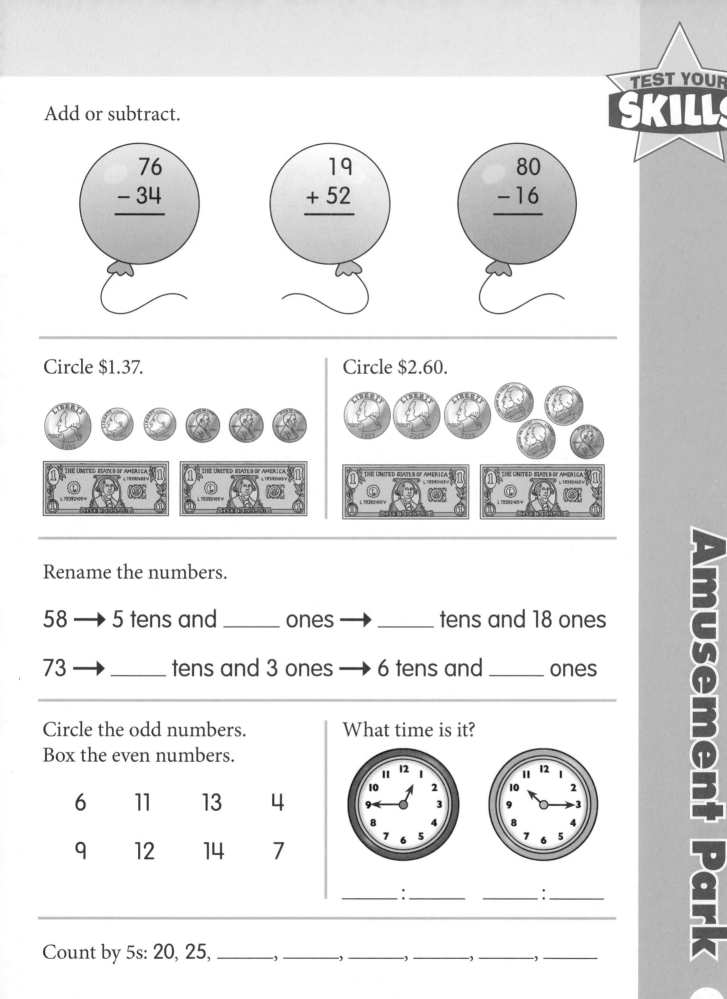

$$\begin{array}{r} 76 \\ -\ 34 \\ \hline \end{array}$$

$$\begin{array}{r} 19 \\ +\ 52 \\ \hline \end{array}$$

$$\begin{array}{r} 80 \\ -\ 16 \\ \hline \end{array}$$

Circle $1.37.

Circle $2.60.

Rename the numbers.

58 → 5 tens and _____ ones → _____ tens and 18 ones

73 → _____ tens and 3 ones → 6 tens and _____ ones

Circle the odd numbers.
Box the even numbers.

6   11   13   4

9   12   14   7

What time is it?

_____ : _____   _____ : _____

Count by 5s: 20, 25, _____, _____, _____, _____, _____, _____

Amusement Park

Skill:
Use addition strategies (regrouping)

Add.

16 + 16 ——— Add the ones.	**1** 16 + 16 ——— 2 Write the ones. Move the tens to the tens place.	**1** 16 + 16 ——— 32 Add the tens.

T	I	A	N	B	F
18 + 8	33 + 29	57 + 18	44 + 28	65 + 15	29 + 29

Y	X	E	O	R	D
15 + 68	77 + 13	19 + 47	38 + 38	16 + 26	54 + 19

Write the letter for each sum to find out when it will rain.

___ ___   ___ ___ ___ ___
80   83   72   66   90   26

___ ___ ___ ___ ___ ___
58   42   62   73   75   83

Weather Watch

Add.

Skill:
Use addition strategies (regrouping)

17	15	18	14	19
+ 7	+ 9	+ 8	+ 9	+ 9

17	19	19	29	36
+ 38	+ 15	+ 53	+ 26	+ 19

28	19	17	39	34
+ 35	+ 75	+ 24	+ 22	+ 57

37	33	25	18	42
+ 19	+ 37	+ 38	+ 37	+ 18

Did you get four answers of **55**?
If you did, color the sun.
If you did not, color the rain.

Weather Watch

How Much Did It Snow?

Skill:
Use subtraction strategies (regrouping)

Subtract.

$$
\begin{array}{r} 34 \\ -\ 6 \\ \hline \end{array}
$$

Subtract the ones. If you can't, regroup.

$$
\begin{array}{r} {}^{2}\cancel{3}{}^{14}\cancel{4} \\ -\ 6 \\ \hline 8 \end{array}
$$

Regroup 30 and 4 as 20 and 14.

$$
\begin{array}{r} {}^{2}\cancel{3}{}^{14}\cancel{4} \\ -\ 6 \\ \hline 28 \end{array}
$$

Subtract 6 from 14 and 0 from 2.

$$
\begin{array}{r} 53 \\ -15 \\ \hline \end{array}
\qquad
\begin{array}{r} 71 \\ -26 \\ \hline \end{array}
\qquad
\begin{array}{r} 32 \\ -24 \\ \hline \end{array}
\qquad
\begin{array}{r} 58 \\ -39 \\ \hline \end{array}
$$

$$
\begin{array}{r} 70 \\ -59 \\ \hline \end{array}
\qquad
\begin{array}{r} 85 \\ -38 \\ \hline \end{array}
\qquad
\begin{array}{r} 94 \\ -87 \\ \hline \end{array}
\qquad
\begin{array}{r} 80 \\ -24 \\ \hline \end{array}
$$

$$
\begin{array}{r} 74 \\ -59 \\ \hline \end{array}
\qquad
\begin{array}{r} 46 \\ -18 \\ \hline \end{array}
\qquad
\begin{array}{r} 75 \\ -57 \\ \hline \end{array}
\qquad
\begin{array}{r} 50 \\ -26 \\ \hline \end{array}
$$

Find out how much it snowed last month. Look at your answers. Circle the number that is greater than 25 but less than 30.

It snowed _____ centimeters.

Skill Sharpeners: Math • EMC 8252 • © Evan-Moor Corp.

Snowman Addition

Add.

Skill:
Add three or more numbers within 200

$$\begin{array}{r} 45 \\ 15 \\ 27 \\ + 32 \\ \hline \end{array}$$

$$\begin{array}{r} 31 \\ 12 \\ 21 \\ + 63 \\ \hline \end{array}$$

$$\begin{array}{r} 12 \\ 23 \\ 34 \\ + 45 \\ \hline \end{array}$$

$$\begin{array}{r} 26 \\ 30 \\ 42 \\ + 10 \\ \hline \end{array}$$

$$\begin{array}{r} 61 \\ 25 \\ 19 \\ + 35 \\ \hline \end{array}$$

$$\begin{array}{r} 52 \\ 30 \\ 25 \\ + 47 \\ \hline \end{array}$$

North Pole

$$\begin{array}{r} 45 \\ 16 \\ 20 \\ + 24 \\ \hline \end{array}$$

Weather Watch

Skill:
Measure length using centimeters

These carrots will be used to make noses for four snowmen. How many centimeters long is each one?

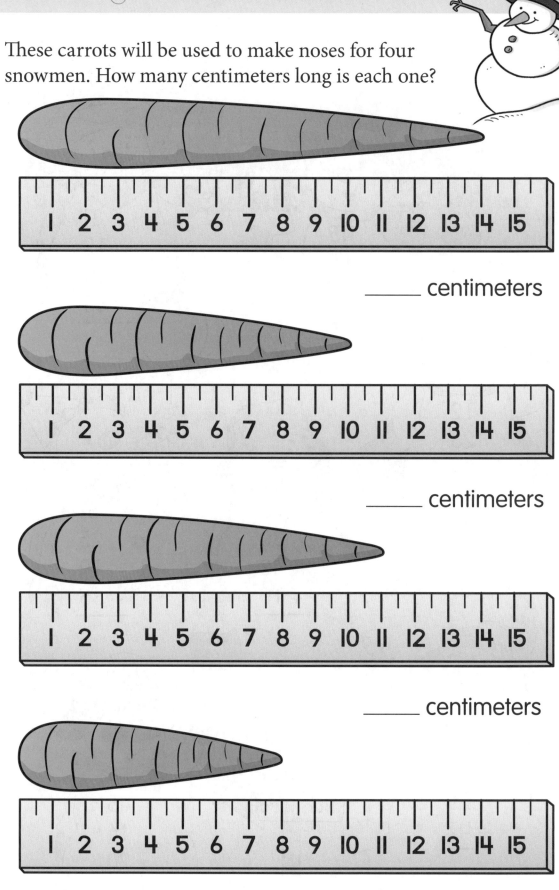

_____ centimeters

_____ centimeters

_____ centimeters

_____ centimeters

Weather Watch

Count by 2s. Write the missing numbers
on the paths to help the children get home.

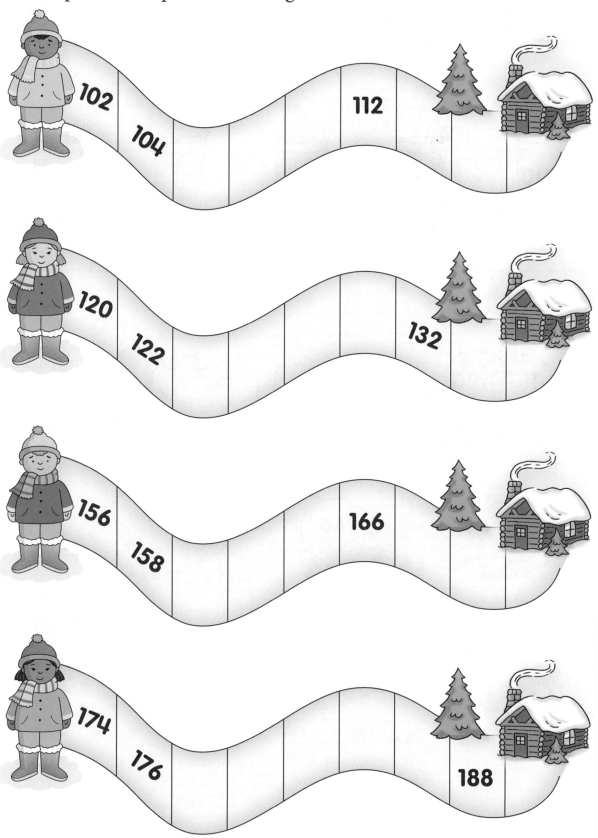

Weather Watch

Ready for the Cold

Skill:
Count by 5s
and 10s

Count by 5s.

105 110

140 145

Count by 10s.

110 120

150 160

Subtract. Then add to check the answers.

Skill:
Recognize relationship between addition and subtraction

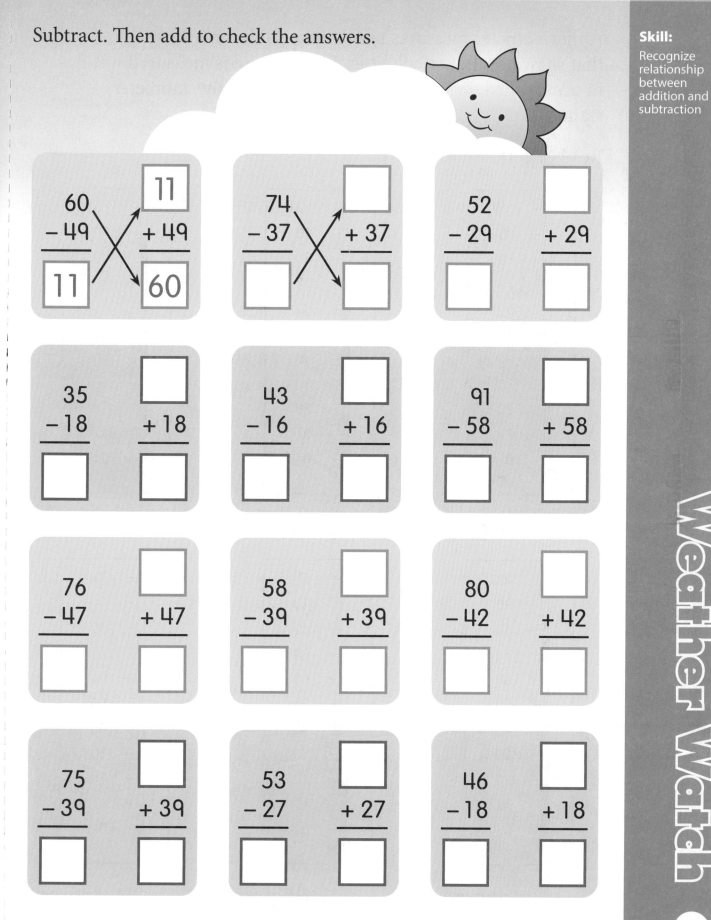

$$\begin{array}{r} 60 \\ -\ 49 \\ \hline \boxed{11} \end{array} \quad \begin{array}{r} \boxed{11} \\ +\ 49 \\ \hline \boxed{60} \end{array}$$

$$\begin{array}{r} 74 \\ -\ 37 \\ \hline \Box \end{array} \quad \begin{array}{r} \Box \\ +\ 37 \\ \hline \Box \end{array}$$

$$\begin{array}{r} 52 \\ -\ 29 \\ \hline \Box \end{array} \quad \begin{array}{r} \Box \\ +\ 29 \\ \hline \Box \end{array}$$

$$\begin{array}{r} 35 \\ -\ 18 \\ \hline \Box \end{array} \quad \begin{array}{r} \Box \\ +\ 18 \\ \hline \Box \end{array}$$

$$\begin{array}{r} 43 \\ -\ 16 \\ \hline \Box \end{array} \quad \begin{array}{r} \Box \\ +\ 16 \\ \hline \Box \end{array}$$

$$\begin{array}{r} 91 \\ -\ 58 \\ \hline \Box \end{array} \quad \begin{array}{r} \Box \\ +\ 58 \\ \hline \Box \end{array}$$

$$\begin{array}{r} 76 \\ -\ 47 \\ \hline \Box \end{array} \quad \begin{array}{r} \Box \\ +\ 47 \\ \hline \Box \end{array}$$

$$\begin{array}{r} 58 \\ -\ 39 \\ \hline \Box \end{array} \quad \begin{array}{r} \Box \\ +\ 39 \\ \hline \Box \end{array}$$

$$\begin{array}{r} 80 \\ -\ 42 \\ \hline \Box \end{array} \quad \begin{array}{r} \Box \\ +\ 42 \\ \hline \Box \end{array}$$

$$\begin{array}{r} 75 \\ -\ 39 \\ \hline \Box \end{array} \quad \begin{array}{r} \Box \\ +\ 39 \\ \hline \Box \end{array}$$

$$\begin{array}{r} 53 \\ -\ 27 \\ \hline \Box \end{array} \quad \begin{array}{r} \Box \\ +\ 27 \\ \hline \Box \end{array}$$

$$\begin{array}{r} 46 \\ -\ 18 \\ \hline \Box \end{array} \quad \begin{array}{r} \Box \\ +\ 18 \\ \hline \Box \end{array}$$

Weather Watch

A thermometer measures temperature. It has markings
that show how hot or cold it is. Temperature is measured
in units called degrees. Each marking on the thermometer
stands for 2 degrees.

Read each thermometer and write the temperature.

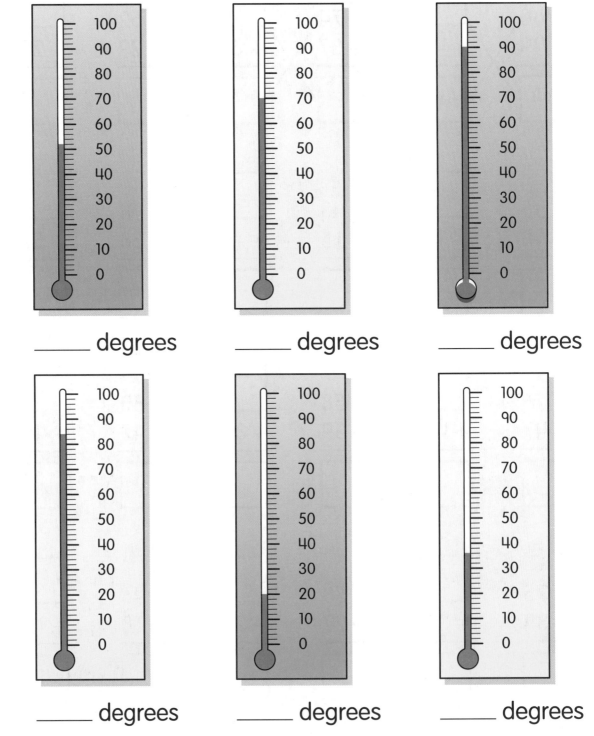

_____ degrees   _____ degrees   _____ degrees

_____ degrees   _____ degrees   _____ degrees

Skill Sharpeners: Math • EMC 8252 • © Evan-Moor Corp.

Solve the problems.

Skills:
Solve word problems; Use addition and subtraction strategies (regrouping)

The temperature in the morning was 58 degrees. In the afternoon it was 12 degrees higher. What was the afternoon temperature?

_____ degrees

It was 54 degrees two hours ago. Now it is 9 degrees warmer. What is the temperature now?

_____ degrees

The temperature at noon was 75 degrees. It dropped 18 degrees in the evening. What was the evening temperature?

_____ degrees

It may snow if the temperature falls to 32 degrees. It is 40 degrees now. How many degrees must the temperature fall for it to snow?

_____ degrees

The hottest temperature of the year was 98 degrees. The coldest was 29 degrees. What was the difference between these two temperatures?

_____ degrees

Amy can't wear shorts until the temperature reaches 65 degrees. It is only 47 degrees now. How much does the temperature need to rise before Amy can wear shorts?

_____ degrees

Weather Watch

Favorite Weather

Some students voted for their favorite kind of weather.

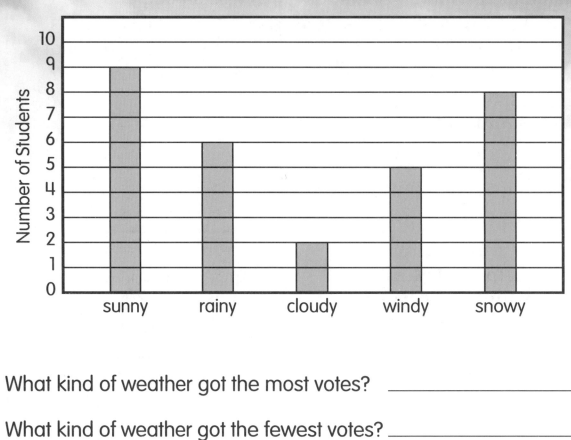

Favorite Weather

What kind of weather got the most votes? _____

What kind of weather got the fewest votes? _____

How many students chose windy weather? _____

How many more students chose snowy
weather than cloudy weather? _____

How many students voted in all? _____

Add or subtract. Fill in the circle to show the answer.

57
+ 23
◯ 80
◯ 70
◯ 14

94
− 48
◯ 48
◯ 46
◯ 56

82
− 53
◯ 39
◯ 31
◯ 29

Write the temperature.

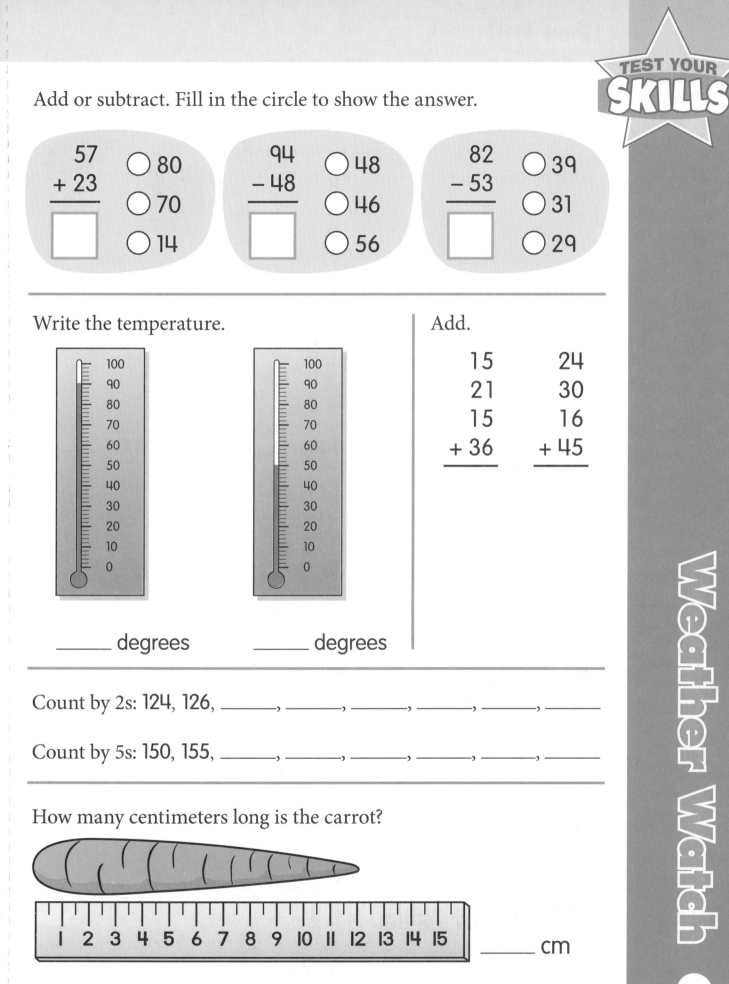

_____ degrees   _____ degrees

Add.

15
21
15
+ 36

24
30
16
+ 45

Count by 2s: 124, 126, _____, _____, _____, _____, _____, _____

Count by 5s: 150, 155, _____, _____, _____, _____, _____, _____

How many centimeters long is the carrot?

1 2 3 4 5 6 7 8 9 10 11 12 13 14 15   _____ cm

Weather Watch

Skill:

Identify hundreds, tens, and ones

Count the hundreds, tens, and ones.
Write how many blocks there are.

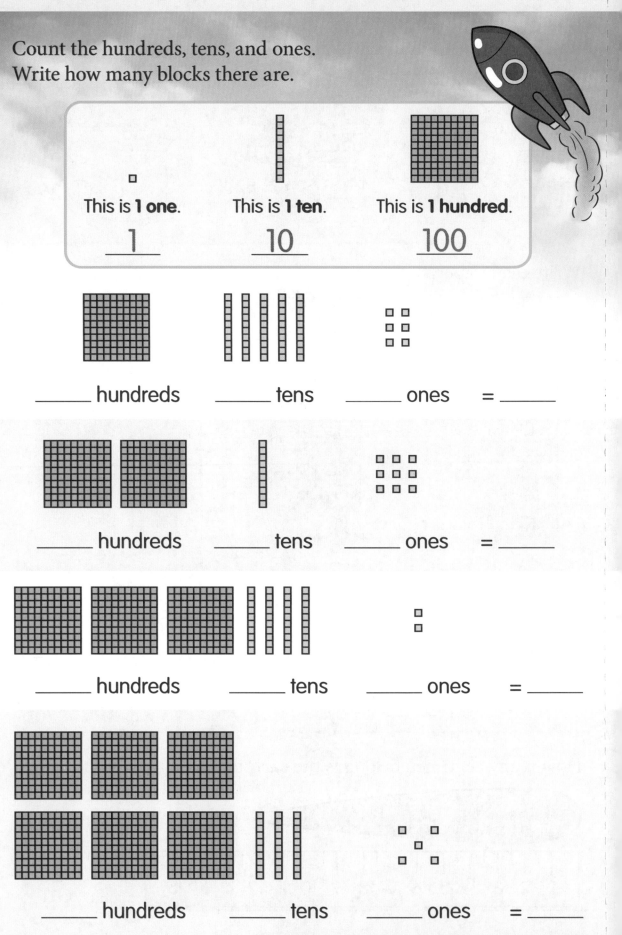

This is **1 one**.
__1__

This is **1 ten**.
__10__

This is **1 hundred**.
__100__

_____ hundreds   _____ tens   _____ ones   = _____

_____ hundreds   _____ tens   _____ ones   = _____

_____ hundreds   _____ tens   _____ ones   = _____

_____ hundreds   _____ tens   _____ ones   = _____

Skill Sharpeners: Math • EMC 8252 • © Evan-Moor Corp.

Skill:

Identify hundreds, tens, and ones

Count the hundreds, tens, and ones.
Write how many blocks there are in all.

hundreds	tens	ones	in all

hundreds	tens	ones	in all

hundreds	tens	ones	in all

hundreds	tens	ones	in all

hundreds	tens	ones	in all

hundreds	tens	ones	in all

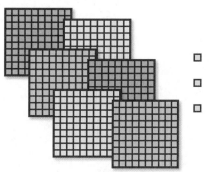

Outer Space

Skill:
Count by 1s within 1,000

Count by 1s. Fill in the paths to help the spaceships get to the planets.

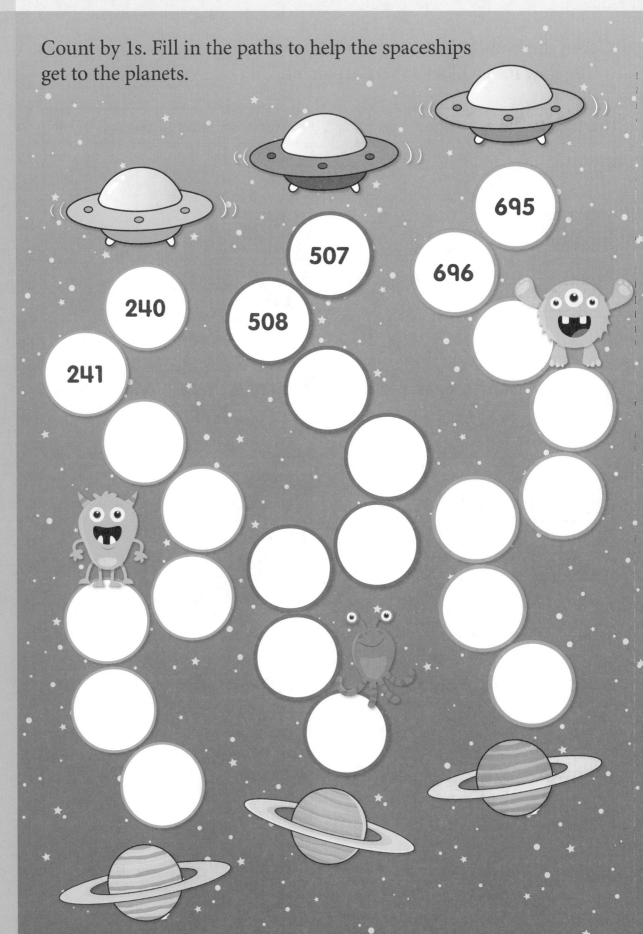

Outer Space

Connect the dots. Start at **179**. Count by 2s.

Skill:
Count by 2s
within 1,000

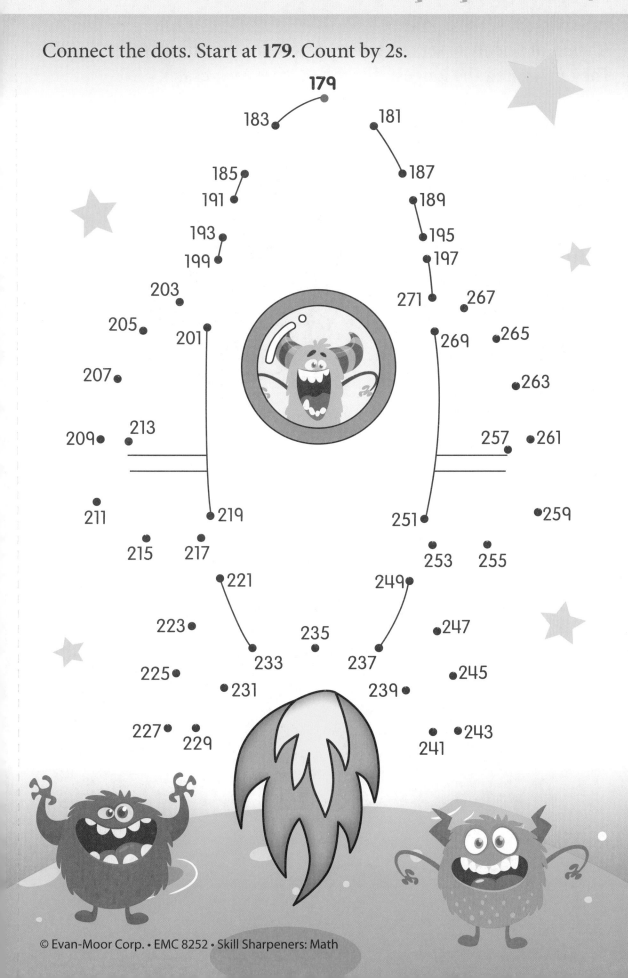

Outer Space

Moon Craters

Skill:
Compare three-digit numbers

A team of scientists set out to measure some moon craters. They measured the longest distance across each crater.

A	698 meters
B	434 meters
C	257 meters
D	643 meters
E	516 meters
F	983 meters
G	850 meters
H	775 meters

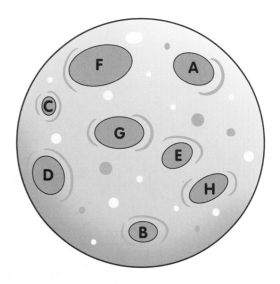

How long was the largest crater? _____ meters

How long was the smallest crater? _____ meters

Which two craters had almost the same length? _____

Which craters were longer than 780 meters? _____

Which crater's measure had 5 in the ones place? _____

Write the number that comes in between.

Skill:
Sequence three-digit numbers

134	_____	136	515	_____	517
301	_____	303	222	_____	224
645	_____	647	715	_____	717
578	_____	580	600	_____	602
832	_____	834	256	_____	258
327	_____	329	483	_____	485
161	_____	163	720	_____	722
929	_____	931	900	_____	902
499	_____	501	199	_____	201
800	_____	802	898	_____	900

Outer Space

A Space Robot

Add.

256 + 142	503 + 364	355 + 210
462 + 517	181 + 407	622 + 156
375 + 303	704 + 163	513 + 142

What was the biggest sum? _____

Outer Space

74

Solve the problems.

Skills:
Solve word problems; Add within 1,000

Rodney Rocketeer flew his spaceship through an asteroid belt. He dodged 175 large asteroids and 203 small ones. How many asteroids did he dodge in all?

_____ asteroids

Rodney kept track of the stars he passed. He counted 104 yesterday and 95 today. How many stars has he passed?

_____ stars

It took Rodney 110 days to reach Planet X. It took another 57 days to reach Planet Y. How many days did it take altogether?

_____ days

Rodney's spaceship travels 320 miles a minute! How far does his ship travel in 2 minutes? How far does it travel in 3 minutes?

_____ miles in 2 minutes

_____ miles in 3 minutes

Outer Space

Use the code to solve the riddle.
Write the matching letter below each answer.

If athletes get athlete's foot, what do astronauts get?

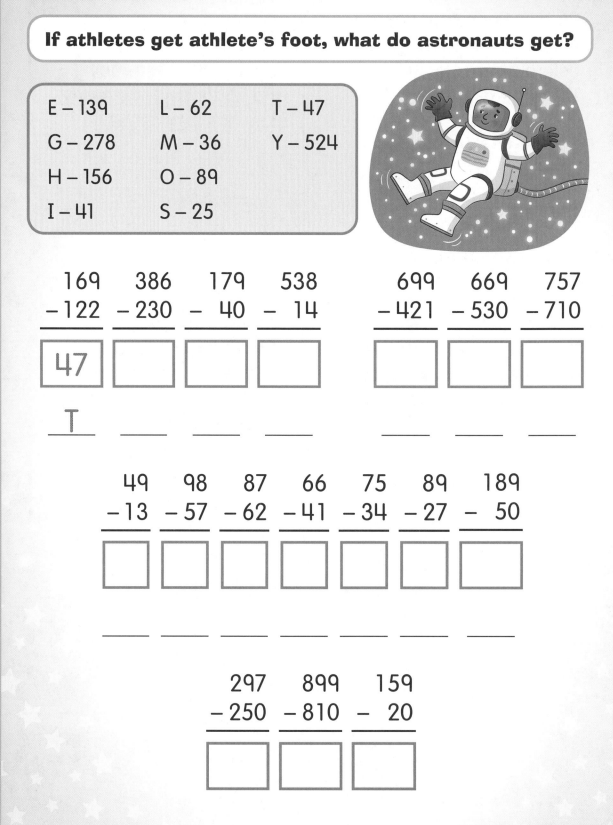

E – 139	L – 62	T – 47
G – 278	M – 36	Y – 524
H – 156	O – 89	
I – 41	S – 25	

| 169 | 386 | 179 | 538 | 699 | 669 | 757 |
| -122 | -230 | - 40 | - 14 | -421 | -530 | -710 |

| **47** | | | | | | |

T __ __ __ __ __ __

| 49 | 98 | 87 | 66 | 75 | 89 | 189 |
| -13 | -57 | -62 | -41 | -34 | -27 | - 50 |

| | | | | | | |

__ __ __ __ __ __ __

| 297 | 899 | 159 |
| -250 | -810 | - 20 |

| | | |

__ __ __

Solve the problems.

Astronaut Ann collected moon rocks.
The largest one weighed 115 pounds. The smallest
weighed 4 pounds. How many pounds heavier was
the largest rock than the smallest?

_____ pounds

Rocket A traveled 247 miles farther than Rocket B. If
Rocket B traveled 731 miles, how far did Rocket A travel?

_____ miles

The temperature on Earth can be as hot as 140 degrees
Fahrenheit. On Venus, it can get 730 degrees hotter than
that! How high can the temperature go on Venus?

_____ degrees

Astronaut Al weighed 180 pounds on Earth and only
30 pounds on the moon! How many pounds heavier
was he on Earth than on the moon?

_____ pounds

It takes Earth 365 days to make a trip around the sun.
It takes Mars 687 days to travel around the sun. How
many days longer does it take Mars than Earth to go
around the sun?

_____ days

© Evan-Moor Corp. • EMC 8252 • Skill Sharpeners: Math

Skills:
Solve word problems; Add and subtract within 1,000

Skill:
Tell time to
the nearest
five minutes

Count by fives around the clock.
Then write the times below.

7:05
5 minutes after 7

7:10
10 minutes after 7

_____ : _____   _____ : _____   _____ : _____   _____ : _____

_____ : _____   _____ : _____   _____ : _____   _____ : _____

Skill:
Tell time to
the nearest
five minutes

The commander of Space Station Seven posted a list of chores to be done and the times they needed to be finished.

Draw lines to match each chore with the correct clock.

Check escape pods   2:15 •

Fill fuel tank   4:10 •

Clean video screens   7:45 •

Check sensors   9:50 •

Charge camera battery   6:10 •

Update space journal   11:55 •

Outer Space

Count the hundreds, tens, and ones.
Write how many blocks there are.

_____ hundreds   _____ tens   _____ ones   = _____

Fill in the missing numbers.

456, 457, _____, _____, _____, _____, _____, _____

What time is it?

_____ : _____   _____ : _____   _____ : _____

Add or subtract.

```
  347        480        693
+ 241       - 20      - 510
```

Solve.

Astronaut Ann will spend 365 days in space. She has been there for 150 days. How many more days will she be there?

_____ days

Skill Sharpeners: Math • EMC 8252 • © Evan-Moor Corp.

Add.

Skill:
Use addition strategies (regrouping)

67
+ 29
―――

19
+ 19
―――

48
+ 31
―――

67
+ 19
―――

58
+ 29
―――

75
+ 19
―――

24
+ 36
―――

73
+ 18
―――

49
+ 29
―――

25
+ 28
―――

77
+ 15
―――

18
+ 38
―――

39
+ 18
―――

45
+ 36
―――

37
+ 28
―――

26
+ 14
―――

Celebration Time

Skills:
Solve word problems; Add and subtract within 100; Add three or more numbers within 100

Here are the prices of some items you might buy for your party. Use the information to help you solve each problem.

balloon $1 **party favor $5** **party hat $2** **noisemaker $3**

If you bought each guest all four party items, how much would you spend for each person?

$_____

If you buy one balloon and one party hat for each guest, how many guests can you invite if you spend $30 on these items?

_____ guests

You have $50 to spend. Can you buy all of the items for 5 guests?

_____

This is what you bought:

🎩 5   🛍 5   🎈 10

How much did you spend?

$_____

Celebration Time

Skill Sharpeners: Math • EMC 8252 • © Evan-Moor Corp.

Write **>** or **<** in each circle to compare the numbers.

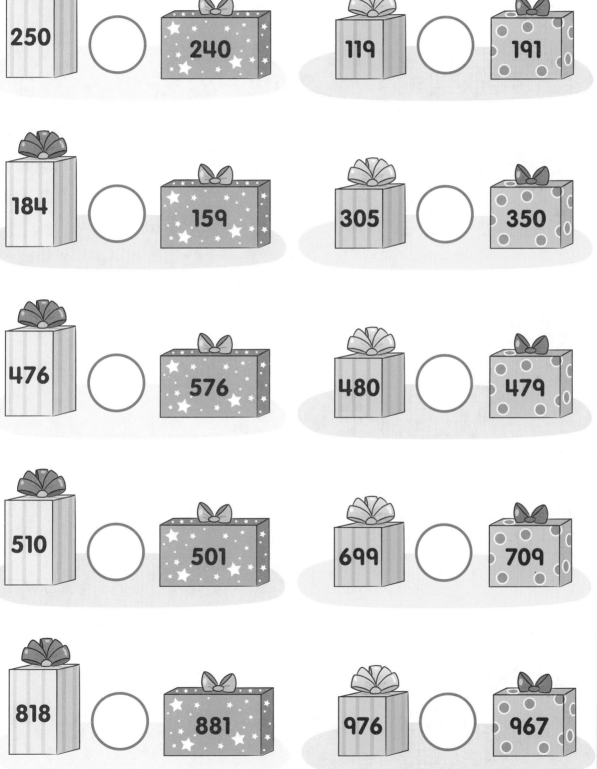

Celebration Time

83

Skill:
Write numbers in expanded form

Write each number in expanded form.

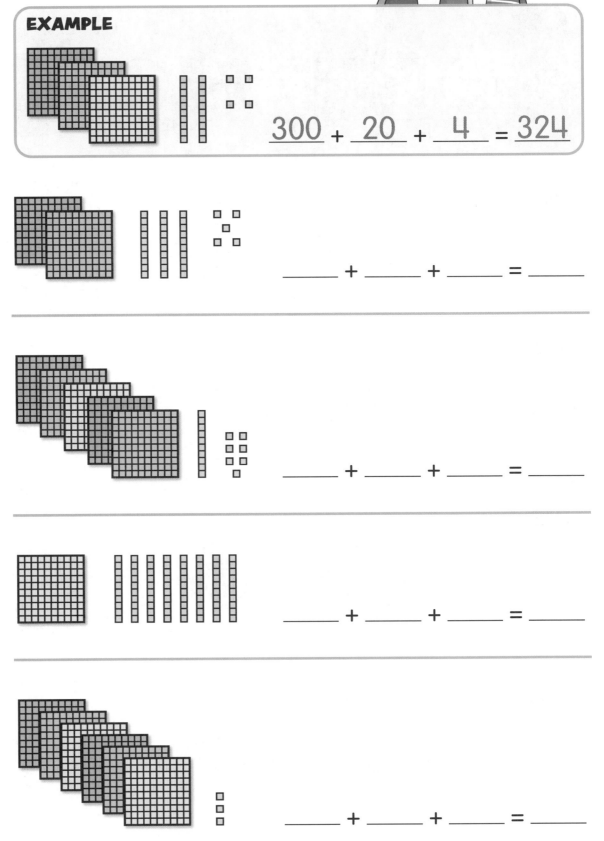

EXAMPLE

$\underline{300} + \underline{20} + \underline{4} = \underline{324}$

_____ + _____ + _____ = _____

_____ + _____ + _____ = _____

_____ + _____ + _____ = _____

_____ + _____ + _____ = _____

Celebration Time

84

Count by 100s. Write the numbers on the hats.

Skill:
Count by 100s

Celebration Time

Skills:
Add equal groups of numbers; Write equations

Count the party treats in each row. Write an addition sentence to show how many there are in all.

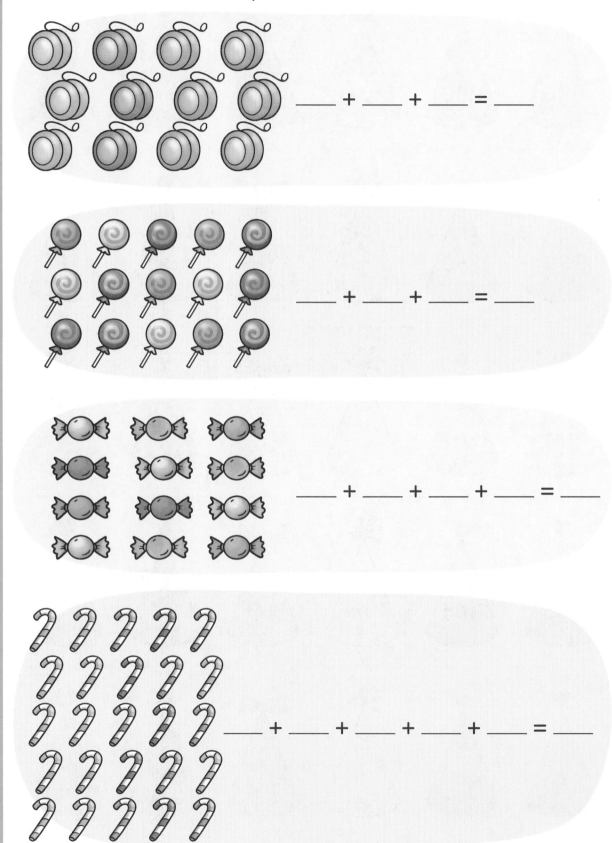

___ + ___ + ___ = ___

___ + ___ + ___ = ___

___ + ___ + ___ + ___ = ___

___ + ___ + ___ + ___ + ___ = ___

Add.

Skill:
Use addition strategies (regrouping)

```
  415          134          258          668
+ 107        + 529        + 235        + 224
```

```
  186          503          724          379
+ 408        + 327        + 216        + 512
```

```
  459          168          824          226
+ 118        + 202        + 158        + 126
```

```
  375          641          857          349
+ 416        + 109        + 137        + 544
```

Celebration Time

Skill:
Use addition strategies (regrouping)

Celebration Time

Add.

256 + 362	381 + 139	582 + 225	446 + 371
755 + 153	742 + 191	371 + 385	590 + 148
762 + 165	483 + 372	559 + 360	133 + 482
183 + 286	476 + 260	214 + 193	562 + 154

Skill Sharpeners: Math • EMC 8252 • © Evan-Moor Corp.

Add.

Skill:
Use addition strategies (regrouping)

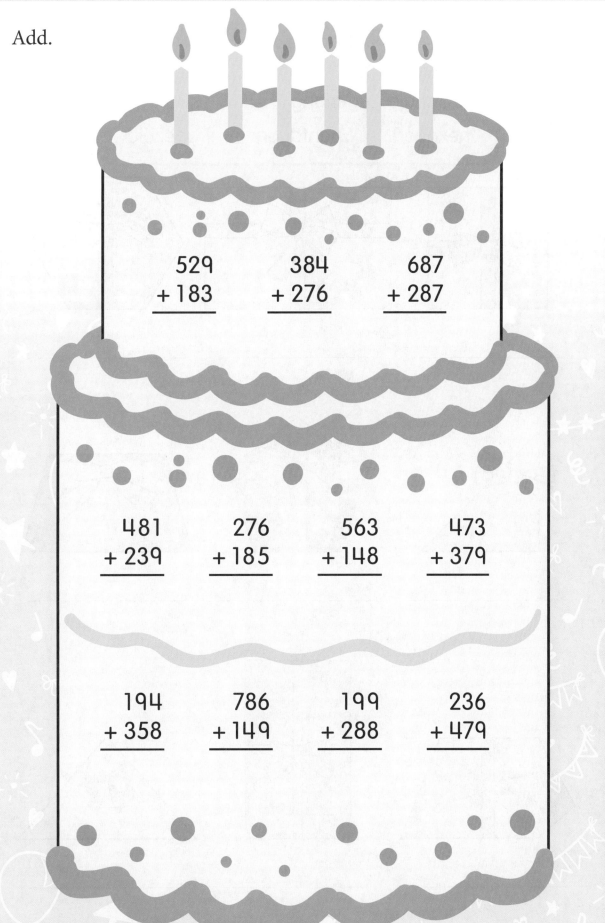

529
+ 183

384
+ 276

687
+ 287

481
+ 239

276
+ 185

563
+ 148

473
+ 379

194
+ 358

786
+ 149

199
+ 288

236
+ 479

Celebration Time

Write the name of each shape.

rectangle   triangle   square

hexagon   pentagon   trapezoid

_____   _____   _____

_____   _____   _____

_____   _____   _____

Skill:
Create a bar graph

We saw these things in the parade:

7 bands	5 balloons	10 floats
4 dogs	3 firetrucks	9 bicycles
11 funny cars	12 dancers	8 horses

Label the graph and color in the boxes to show the information from above.

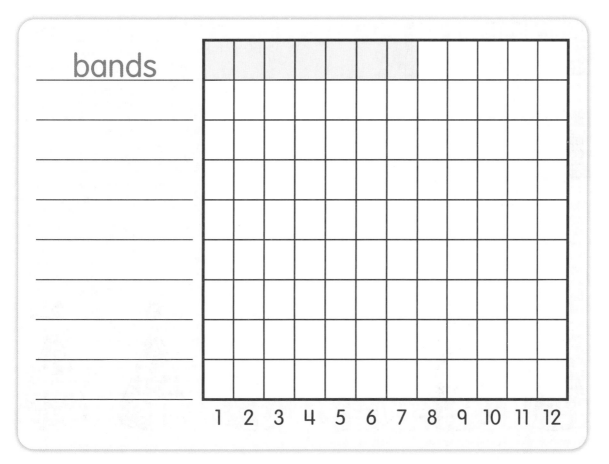

bands

1 2 3 4 5 6 7 8 9 10 11 12

Celebration Time

Add.

$$723 + 145$$ $$216 + 136$$ $$409 + 387$$ $$164 + 185$$ $$531 + 286$$

Write each number in expanded form.

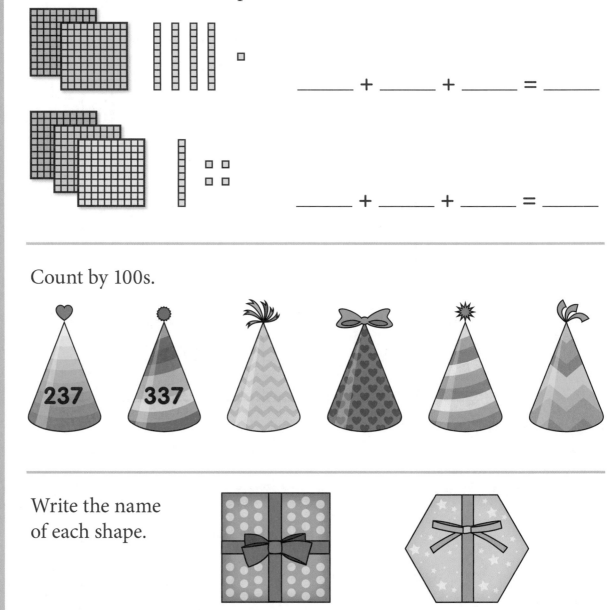

_____ + _____ + _____ = _____

_____ + _____ + _____ = _____

Count by 100s.

237   337

Write the name of each shape.

_____   _____

Skill Sharpeners: Math • EMC 8252 • © Evan-Moor Corp.

Skill:
Identify equal shares

Find the shapes that show one half shaded. Circle them in **blue**. Circle the shapes that show one third in **green**. Circle the shapes that show one fourth in **red**. Connect the green circles to make a trail for the giraffe to reach the watering hole.

Animals, Animals

Skill:
Identify odd and
even numbers

Circle two at a time. Write **odd** or **even**.

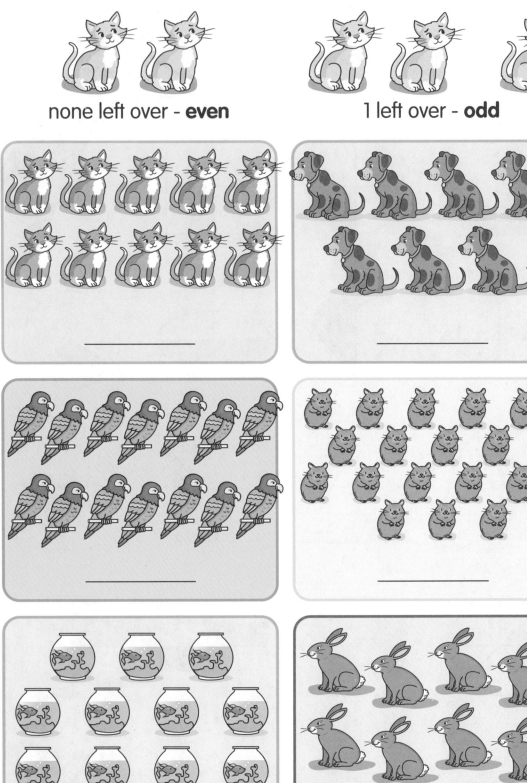

none left over - **even**

1 left over - **odd**

Animals, Animals

Skill Sharpeners: Math • EMC 8252 • © Evan-Moor Corp.

Color **odd** numbers **green**.
Some odd numbers are 1, 3, 5, 7, and 9.

Color **even** numbers **blue**.
Some even numbers are 2, 4, 6, 8, and 10.

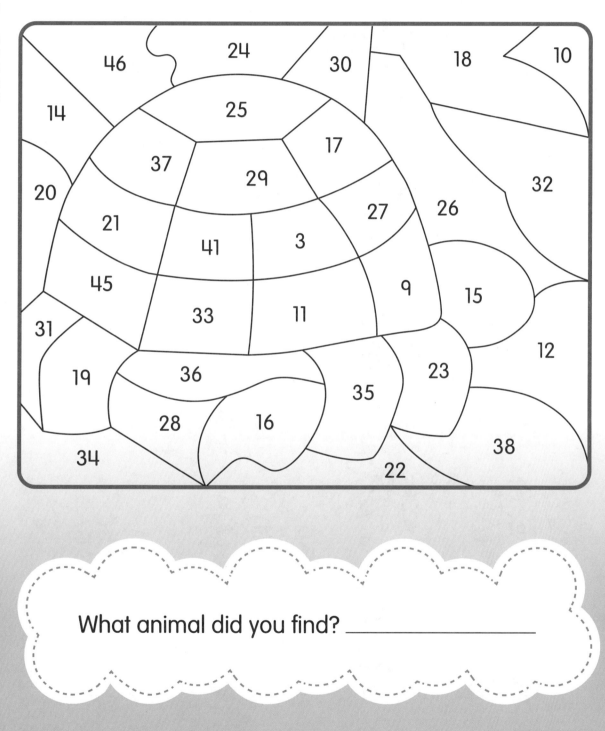

What animal did you find? _____

Animals, Animals

Heading Home

Skill:
Count by 10s

Help Buzz find his way back to the hive. Start at 96. Count by 10s and connect the flowers that Buzz visits.

Animals, Animals

Skill Sharpeners: Math • EMC 8252 • © Evan-Moor Corp.

Count by 5s. Write the numbers on the path to show the cow how to get to the barn.

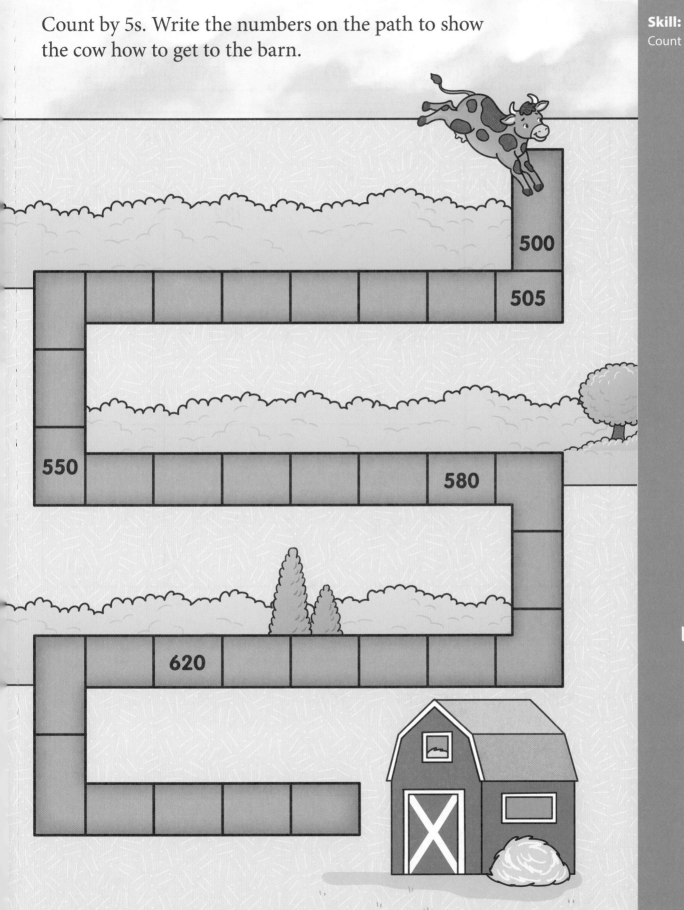

500

505

550

580

620

Animals, Animals

What Is Hiding Here?

Skill:
Compare three-digit numbers

Color the spaces to find the animal living here.

> Greater than 500: **brown**   Less than 500: **blue**

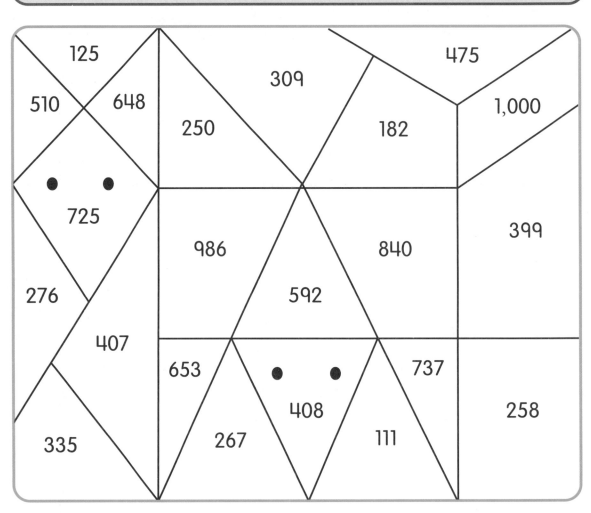

Circle the animal you found.

rabbit   hamster   fox

Skill Sharpeners: Math • EMC 8252 • © Evan-Moor Corp.

Use the code to solve the riddle. Write the matching letter below each answer.

What is the opposite of a cool cat?

629 – g	478 – d	526 – t
534 – a	587 – o	981 – h

218
+ 316

867
+ 114

429
+ 158

388
+ 138

349
+ 129

239
+ 348

365
+ 264

[ ]   [ ] [ ] [ ]   [ ] [ ] [ ]

___   ___ ___ ___   ___ ___ ___

Draw your answer here.

Animals, Animals

Chicken Capers

Skills:
Solve multistep
word problems;
Add and subtract
within 100;
Use addition
and subtraction
strategies
(regrouping)

Solve each problem.

Squawk weighs 5 pounds.
Chester weighs 6 pounds
more than Squawk. How
much do they weigh
together?

_____ pounds

Three hens laid 69 eggs
in all. Henny laid 20 eggs,
and Pepper laid 24 eggs.
How many eggs did
Clucky lay?

_____ eggs

Farmer Jo has 50 pounds
of feed. She feeds her
chickens 16 pounds every
week. How many pounds
will she have left after two
weeks?

_____ pounds

Last week Farmer Sam
made $150 selling eggs.
This week he made $20
more than last week.
How much money did he
make in the two weeks?

$_____

A farmer made pens with different shapes for her animals. Write the name of each shape. Use the words from the box. Then write how many sides, vertices, and angles each shape has.

triangle
quadrilateral
pentagon
hexagon

Skills:
Recognize two-dimensional shapes; Identify attributes of two-dimensional shapes

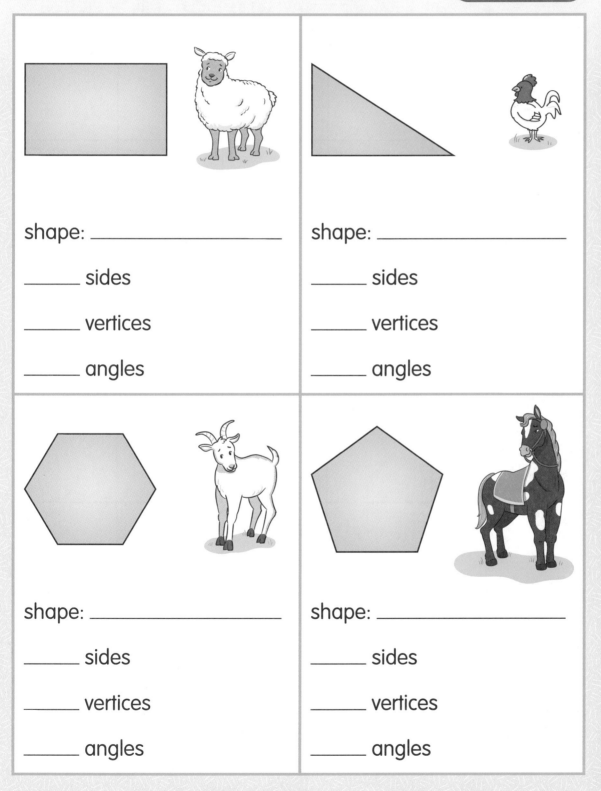

shape: _____

_____ sides

_____ vertices

_____ angles

shape: _____

_____ sides

_____ vertices

_____ angles

shape: _____

_____ sides

_____ vertices

_____ angles

shape: _____

_____ sides

_____ vertices

_____ angles

Animals, Animals

Sticker Buys

Skill:
Calculate amounts with coins

Devon collects stickers of animals. Write how many coins he can use to buy the stickers below. Show the fewest coins each time.

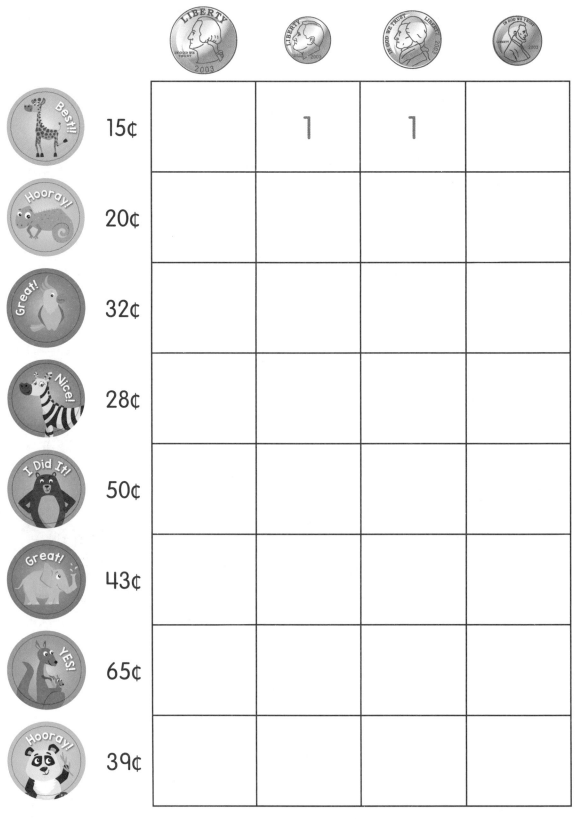

Sticker	(quarter)	(dime)	(nickel)	(penny)
15¢		1	1	
20¢				
32¢				
28¢				
50¢				
43¢				
65¢				
39¢				

Write the length of each creature.

Skill:
Measure length
using inches

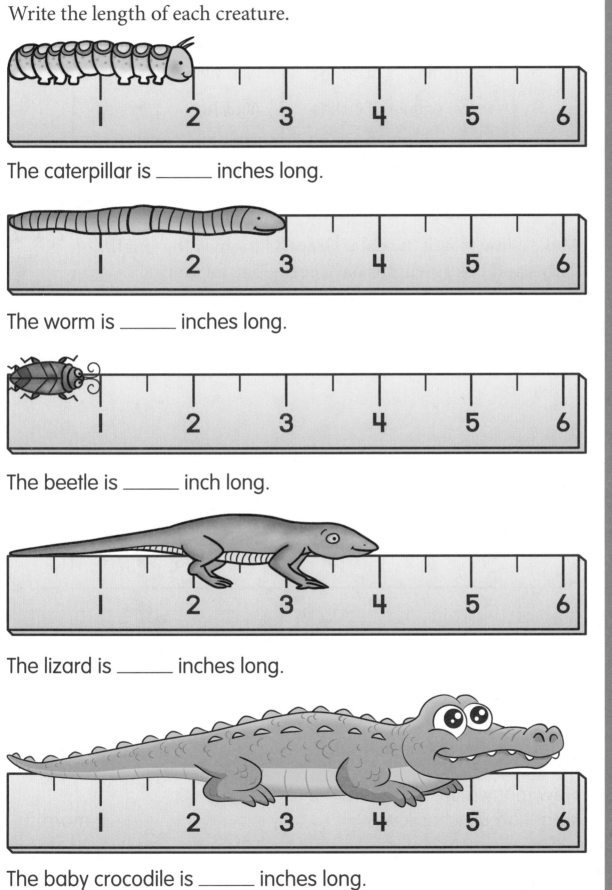

The caterpillar is _____ inches long.

The worm is _____ inches long.

The beetle is _____ inch long.

The lizard is _____ inches long.

The baby crocodile is _____ inches long.

Animals, Animals

Skill:
Create and interpret a line plot

Tomika measured the length of her toy animals.

Tilly Turtle	4 inches	Willy Worm	4 inches
Poky Penguin	4 inches	Atlas Ant	2 inches
Lizzy Lizard	5 inches	Finley Fish	5 inches
Slippy Snake	6 inches	Silky Spider	2 inches

Make a line plot of the data. Draw **X**s to show the lengths. Tilly's and Poky's lengths have been done for you.

Length of Toy Animals

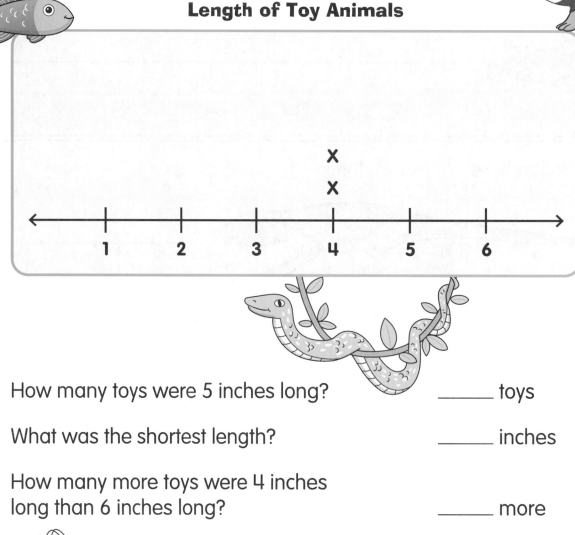

How many toys were 5 inches long? _____ toys

What was the shortest length? _____ inches

How many more toys were 4 inches long than 6 inches long? _____ more

Animals, Animals

Write **half**, **third**, or **fourth** to describe the shaded part.

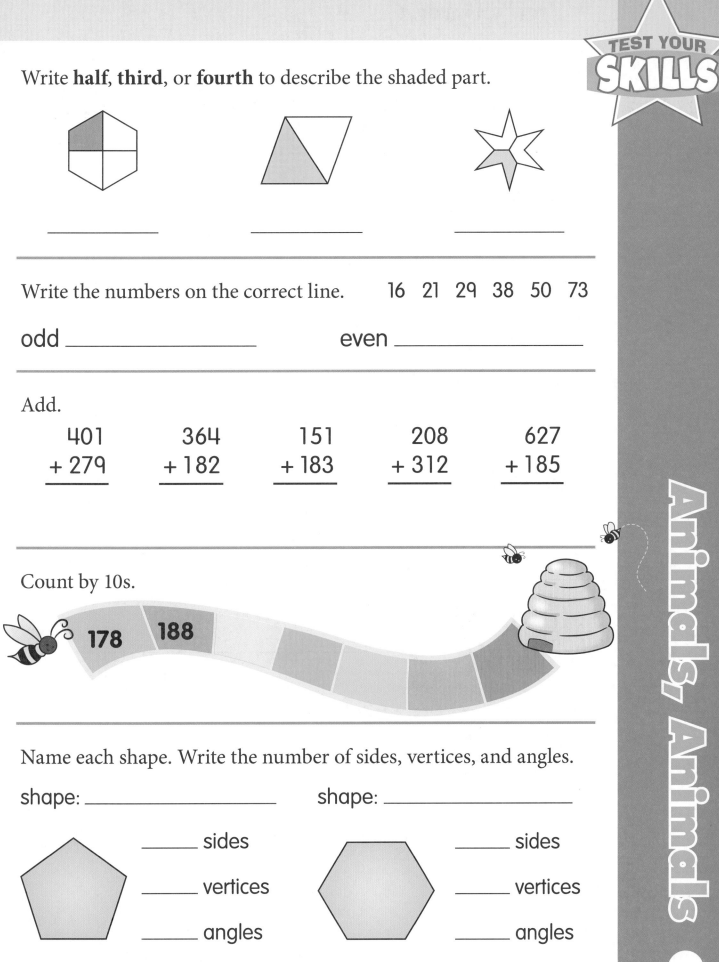

_____   _____   _____

Write the numbers on the correct line.   16   21   29   38   50   73

odd _____   even _____

Add.

401	364	151	208	627
+ 279	+ 182	+ 183	+ 312	+ 185

Count by 10s.

178   **188**

Name each shape. Write the number of sides, vertices, and angles.

shape: _____   shape: _____

_____ sides   _____ sides

_____ vertices   _____ vertices

_____ angles   _____ angles

Animals, Animals

A Pretty Garden

Use the digits in the flowers to make 6 three-digit numbers. List the numbers on the lines in order from the least to the greatest.

Skill Sharpeners: Math • EMC 8252 • © Evan-Moor Corp.

In the Garden

Skill:
Use subtraction strategies (regrouping)

Sometimes you need to regroup to subtract. Solve the problems below. Use the place value blocks to help you.

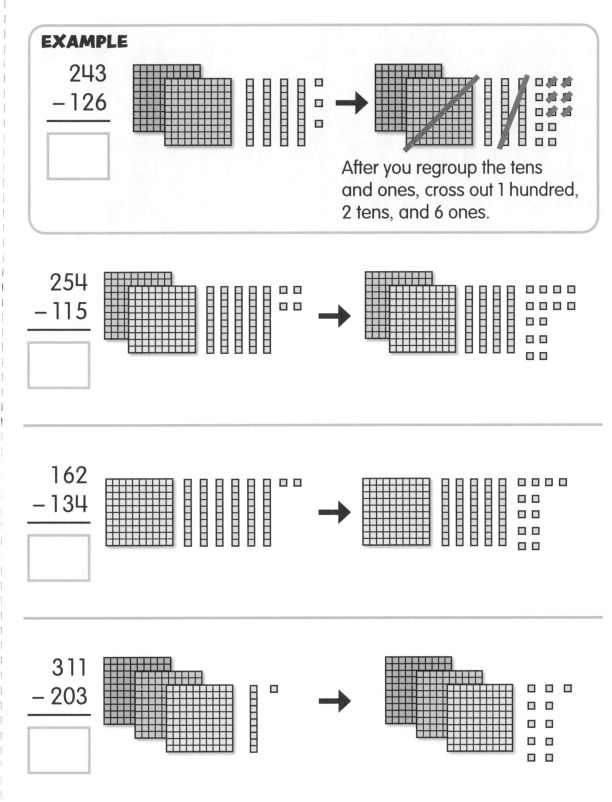

EXAMPLE

243
−126
☐

After you regroup the tens and ones, cross out 1 hundred, 2 tens, and 6 ones.

254
−115
☐

162
−134
☐

311
−203
☐

In the Garden

A Garden Riddle

Use the code to solve the riddle. Write the matching letter below each answer.

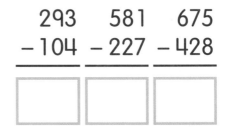

You throw away the outside and cook the inside. Then you eat the outside and throw away the inside. What is it?

354 – A	189 – E	418 – N	247 – R
427 – C	259 – F	571 – O	

$$\begin{array}{cc} 492 & 757 \\ -138 & -339 \end{array}$$

□ □

___ ___

$$\begin{array}{ccc} 293 & 581 & 675 \\ -104 & -227 & -428 \end{array}$$

□ □ □

___ ___ ___

$$\begin{array}{cc} 830 & 378 \\ -259 & -119 \end{array}$$

□ □

___ ___

$$\begin{array}{cccc} 795 & 680 & 376 & 874 \\ -368 & -109 & -129 & -456 \end{array}$$

□ □ □ □

___ ___ ___ ___

In the Garden

108

Skill Sharpeners: Math • EMC 8252 • © Evan-Moor Corp.

Skill:
Use subtraction strategies (regrouping)

Subtract.

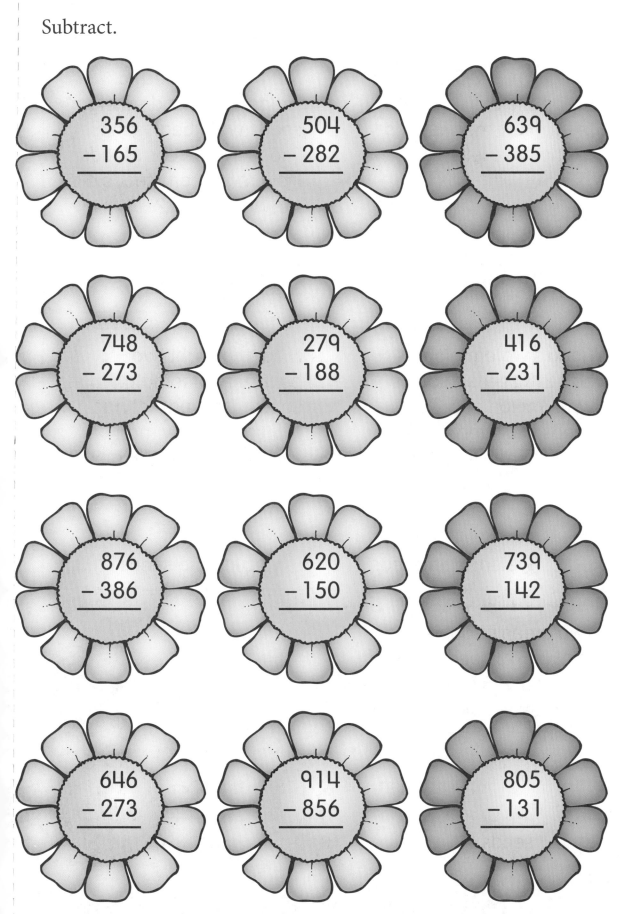

356
−165

504
−282

639
−385

748
−273

279
−188

416
−231

876
−386

620
−150

739
−142

646
−273

914
−856

805
−131

In the Garden

Seed Count

Write an equation for each problem. Then solve it.

Marcus had 215 pumpkin seeds. He planted 46 of them. How many seeds did he have left?

_____ pumpkin seeds

Mr. Wong planted 163 seeds. One hundred eight seeds were bean seeds. The rest were corn seeds. How many corn seeds did Mr. Wong plant?

_____ corn seeds

Fiona's watermelon had 218 seeds. Aiden's watermelon had 226 seeds. How many seeds were there altogether?

_____ watermelon seeds

Megan bought two packages of tomato seeds. Each packet had 165 seeds. How many seeds were there in all?

_____ tomato seeds

Two green peppers had a total of 523 seeds. One of them had 237 seeds. How many seeds did the other green pepper have?

_____ seeds

In the Garden

Skills:
Recognize two-dimensional shapes; Identify attributes of two-dimensional shapes

Korban is planning a garden. He wants it to be in the shape of a quadrilateral. Color all the shapes that show what Korban's garden could look like.

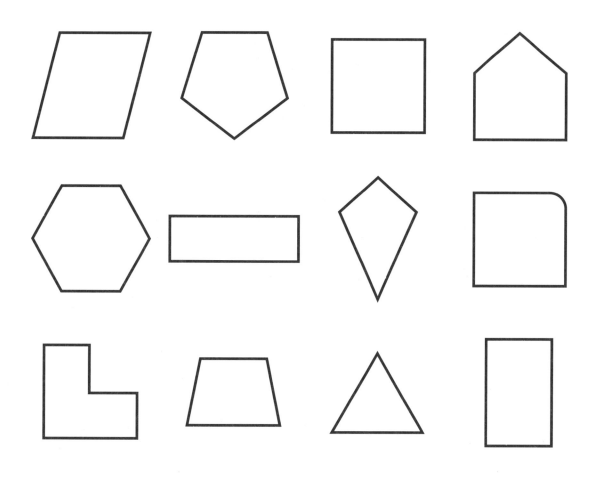

Suppose Korban decides that he wants all sides of the garden to be the same length. Which shape from above would he choose? Draw your answer in the space to the right.

In the Garden

What Time Is It?

Skill:
Tell time to
the nearest
5 minutes

Write the times.

_____ : _____   _____ : _____   _____ : _____

_____ : _____   _____ : _____   _____ : _____

_____ : _____   _____ : _____   _____ : _____

_____ : _____   _____ : _____   _____ : _____

Skill Sharpeners: Math • EMC 8252 • © Evan-Moor Corp.

Skills:
Read a picture graph; Write equations

Teddy went on a bug hunt. The graph shows what he found.

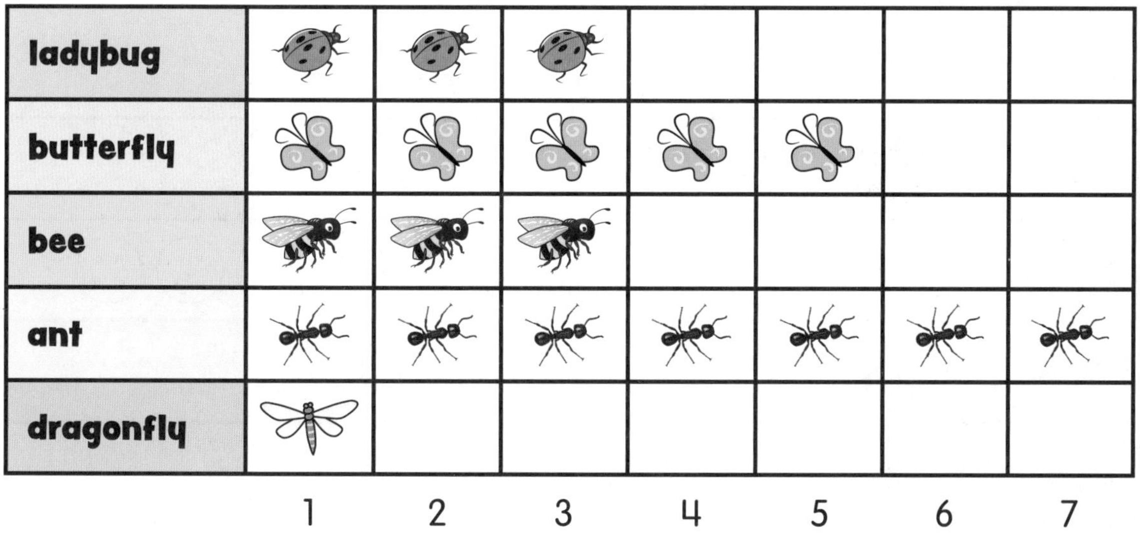

	1	2	3	4	5	6	7
ladybug	🐞	🐞	🐞				
butterfly	🦋	🦋	🦋	🦋	🦋		
bee	🐝	🐝	🐝				
ant	🐜	🐜	🐜	🐜	🐜	🐜	🐜
dragonfly	🪰						

Which insect did Teddy see the most of? How many did he see?

_____

Which insect did Teddy see the fewest of? How many did he see?

_____

How many more butterflies than bees did Teddy see? Show the number sentence.

_____ − _____ = _____

How many ants and ladybugs did Teddy see? Show the number sentence.

_____ + _____ = _____

How many more ants than bees did Teddy see? Show the number sentence.

_____ − _____ = _____

Write a new question about the graph.

_____

_____

In the Garden

Skill:
Read a picture graph

Some children voted for their favorite flower.
The graph shows the flowers they chose.

Favorite Flowers

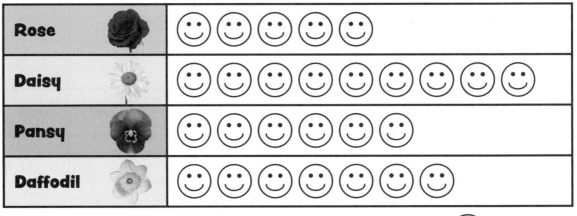

 = 1 vote

How many children chose the pansy? _____

How many children chose the rose? _____

How many more children chose the daffodil than
the rose? _____

Which flower did the most children choose? _____

How many more votes did the most popular flower
get than the least popular flower? _____

In the Garden

Skill Sharpeners: Math • EMC 8252 • © Evan-Moor Corp.

Billy planted beans in his garden. After a while, he measured the plants. He made a line plot showing how tall they were.

Skill:
Read a line plot

Height of Bean Plants in Inches

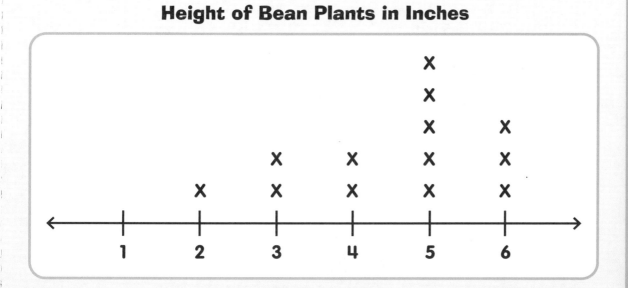

What was the tallest height? _____ inches

What was the shortest height? _____ inches

How many plants were 4 inches tall? _____ plants

Which height did Billy measure most often? _____ inches

How many of the plants were over 4 inches tall? _____ plants

In the Garden

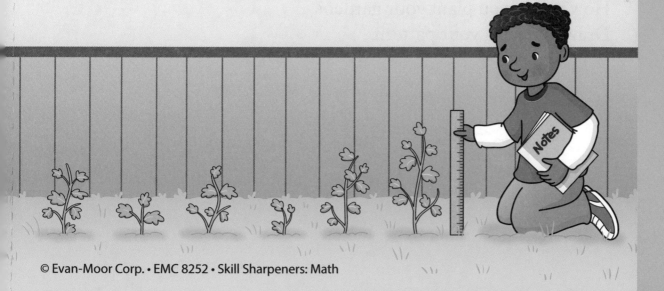

Skill:
Identify and create graphic patterns

A gardener planted vegetables in rows to make patterns.
Use **A**, **B**, and **C** to describe each pattern. The first one has been started for you.

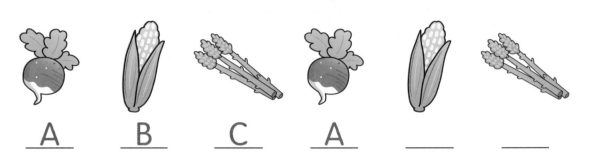

A   B   C   A   ___   ___

___ ___ ___ ___ ___ ___ ___ ___ ___ ___

___ ___ ___ ___ ___ ___ ___ ___

How would you plant your garden?
Draw and label your pattern.

Skill Sharpeners: Math • EMC 8252 • © Evan-Moor Corp.

Subtract.

345	557	476	839	705
−126	−209	−357	−256	−441

Read and solve the problem.

Lam's pumpkin and Jasmine's pumpkin had a total of 417 seeds. Jasmine's had 208 seeds. How many seeds did Lam's pumpkin have?

_____ seeds

What time is it?

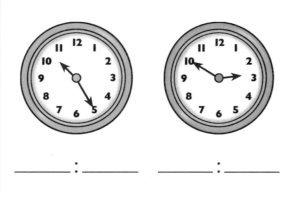

_____ : _____   _____ : _____

Make as many three-digit numbers as you can using the numbers on the flowers. Write them in order from the least to the greatest.

_____, _____, _____, _____, _____, _____

Use the line plot to answer the question.

How tall are the tallest bean plants?

_____ inches

Height of Bean Plants in Inches

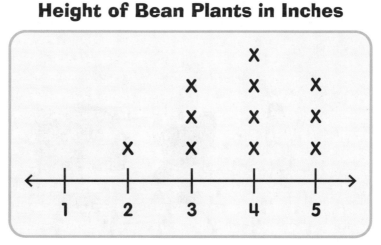

In the Garden

Skills:
Add and subtract within 20; Add three or more numbers within 20

Add or subtract.

9 + 9	5 + 8	13 − 4	8 + 4	14 − 5	18 − 9
16 − 8	8 + 7	14 − 6	7 + 6	9 + 6	15 − 9
13 − 6	12 − 3	9 + 4	7 + 9	9 + 5	15 − 6
16 − 7	13 − 5	17 − 8	8 − 8	4 + 9	12 − 8
9 5 + 1	8 4 + 2	7 7 + 4	9 8 + 0	4 9 + 4	6 3 + 4

Skill Sharpeners: Math • EMC 8252 • © Evan-Moor Corp.

The Beautiful Sea

Skill:
Use addition and subtraction strategies (regrouping)

Add or subtract.

20 + 60	19 + 22	55 + 35	10 + 81	29 + 39

38 − 21	44 − 32	32 − 13	43 − 27	97 − 19	45 − 26

72 − 27	66 + 26	52 + 47	66 − 22	43 − 29	55 − 49

77 − 27	76 + 18	38 + 27	30 − 11	33 − 25	80 − 11

68 − 21	71 + 19	50 − 34	37 + 37	45 + 24	29 − 10

The Beautiful Sea

Skill:
Use addition and subtraction strategies (regrouping)

Use the code to solve the riddle. Write the matching letter below each answer.

> **I am a strange-looking fish. My head looks like a tool that is used for building things. What am I?**

85 – A	92 – D	76 – E	46 – H
59 – K	27 – M	38 – R	63 – S

$$94 - 48 \qquad 49 + 36 \qquad 76 - 49 \qquad 64 - 37 \qquad 48 + 28 \qquad 84 - 46$$

☐ ☐ ☐ ☐ ☐ ☐

___ ___ ___ ___ ___ ___ —

$$82 - 36 \quad 37 + 39 \quad 47 + 38 \quad 64 + 28 \qquad 25 + 38 \quad 63 - 17 \quad 26 + 59 \quad 90 - 52 \quad 92 - 33$$

☐ ☐ ☐ ☐   ☐ ☐ ☐ ☐ ☐

___ ___ ___ ___ ___ ___ ___ ___ ___

Which one do I look like?

The Beautiful Sea

Add or subtract.

Skill:
Use addition and subtraction strategies (regrouping)

$$689 - 465$$

$$655 - 324$$

$$735 - 123$$

$$252 + 346$$

$$405 + 550$$

$$721 + 75$$

$$459 - 379$$

$$953 - 345$$

$$777 - 453$$

$$108 + 392$$

$$263 + 386$$

$$678 + 137$$

$$687 - 445$$

$$153 + 443$$

$$692 - 285$$

$$314 + 297$$

The Beautiful Sea

Solve the problems.

There were 3 groups of whales. There were 18 whales in each group. How many whales were there in all?

_____ whales

There were 134 crabs sitting on the beach. A big wave took 16 crabs out to sea. How many crabs were left on the beach?

_____ crabs

There were 185 mussels covering two rocks. One rock had 108 mussels. How many mussels were on the other rock?

_____ mussels

A seal dove 312 feet into the sea. A second seal dove 408 feet into the sea. How much deeper was the second seal's dive?

_____ feet deeper

A shark swam 39 miles on the first day. It swam 2 more miles on the second day than on the first day. How many miles did the shark travel in the two days?

_____ miles

There were 275 red fish. There were 20 more blue fish than red fish. How many fish were there in all?

_____ fish

Skill:
Calculate amounts with coins

The Seaside Shop sells beautiful shells. Some are shown below. Circle the coins you would use to buy each one. Circle the fewest number possible each time.

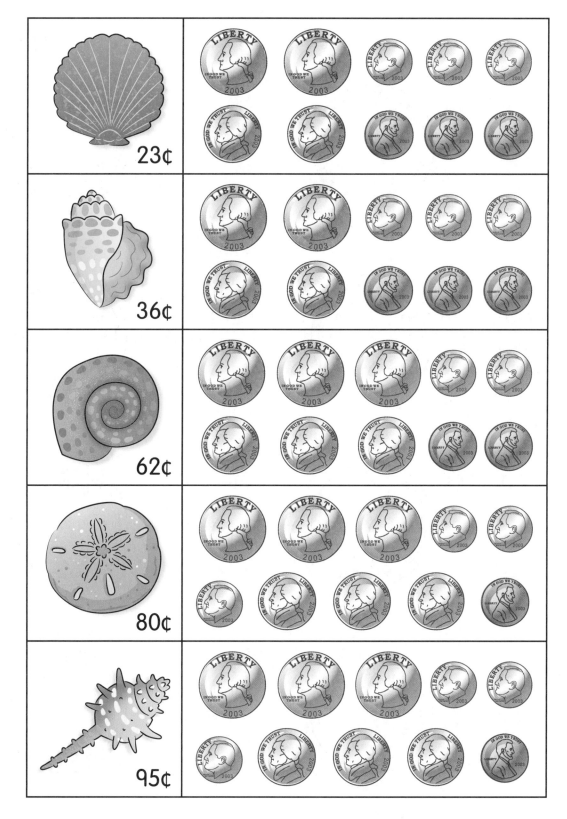

The Beautiful Sea

Fishing Fun

Seth went fishing on the weekend.
Write the time when he did each activity.
Use **a.m.** to show a time before noon.
Use **p.m.** to show a time in the afternoon.

Seth woke up early to go fishing.

7:05 a.m.

He ate ham and eggs for breakfast.

_____

He got to the dock and got in the boat.

_____

Just before lunch, Seth caught a fish!

_____

Seth and his family ate lunch.

_____

After lunch, Seth caught a fish!

_____

Seth got home late in the afternoon.

_____

Seth and his family ate fish for dinner!

_____

Skills:
Tell time to the nearest 5 minutes; Use a.m. and p.m.

The Beautiful Sea

Someone is getting ready to wake up.
Connect the dots to see who it is!
Start at the fish labeled 25. Count by 5s.

Skill:
Count by 5s

What animal do you see? _____

The Beautiful Sea

Skill:

Identify attributes of two- and three-dimensional shapes

Some crabs are playing a game. They are going to crawl to different shapes. Read the clues. Circle the shapes to show where each crab will go.

This crab will crawl only to shapes that have straight sides.

This crab will crawl only to shapes with curved sides.

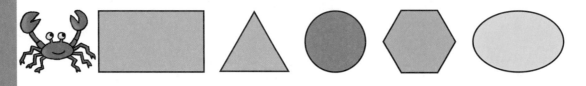

This crab will crawl only to shapes that have corners.

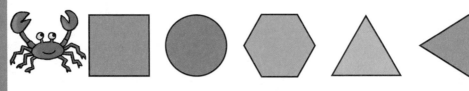

This crab will crawl only to shapes that can roll.

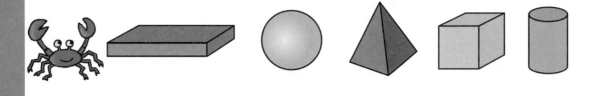

This crab will crawl only to shapes that can be stacked.

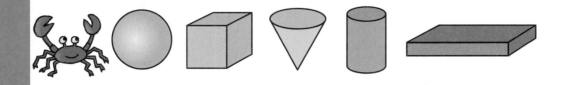

The Beautiful Sea

Skill Sharpeners: Math • EMC 8252 • © Evan-Moor Corp.

How far did each sea snail travel?

Skill:
Measure length using centimeters

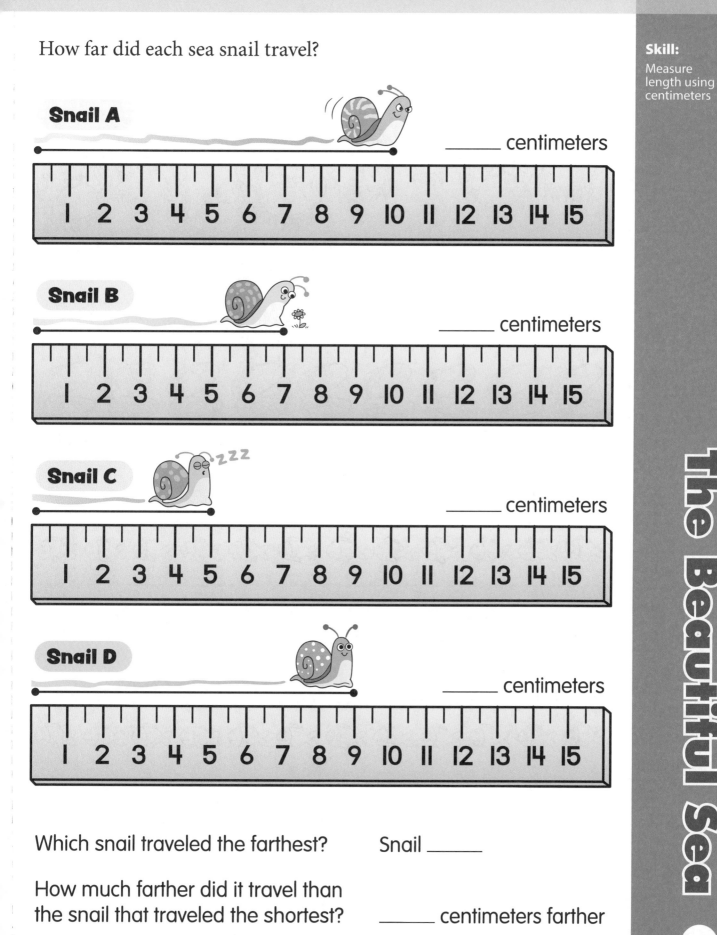

Snail A

_____ centimeters

| 1 | 2 | 3 | 4 | 5 | 6 | 7 | 8 | 9 | 10 | 11 | 12 | 13 | 14 | 15 |

Snail B

_____ centimeters

| 1 | 2 | 3 | 4 | 5 | 6 | 7 | 8 | 9 | 10 | 11 | 12 | 13 | 14 | 15 |

Snail C

_____ centimeters

| 1 | 2 | 3 | 4 | 5 | 6 | 7 | 8 | 9 | 10 | 11 | 12 | 13 | 14 | 15 |

Snail D

_____ centimeters

| 1 | 2 | 3 | 4 | 5 | 6 | 7 | 8 | 9 | 10 | 11 | 12 | 13 | 14 | 15 |

The Beautiful Sea

Which snail traveled the farthest?   Snail _____

How much farther did it travel than
the snail that traveled the shortest?   _____ centimeters farther

Color each set of sea animals to show the patterns.

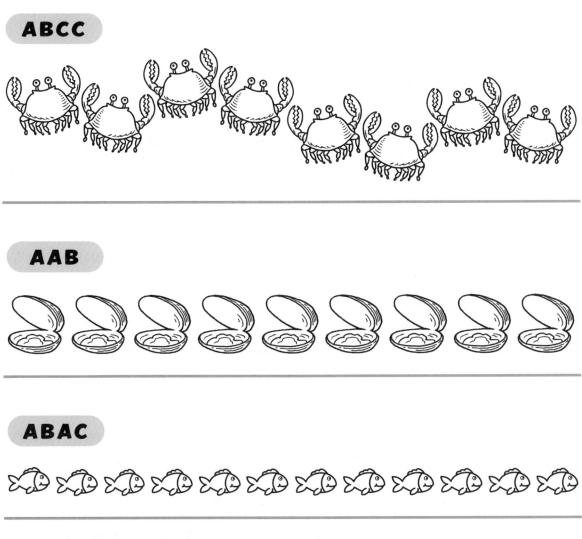

ABCC

AAB

ABAC

Use letters to make your own undersea pattern.
Then color the fish to match.

pattern: _____

The Beautiful Sea

Finish the number patterns. Then write the rule in the boxes.

Skill:
Identify and extend number patterns

__1__ __3__ __5__ __7__ ___ ___ ___ ___

| +2 | +2 | | | | | |

__15__ __13__ __11__ ___ ___ ___ ___

| −2 | | | | | | |

__1__ __6__ __5__ __10__ __9__ ___ ___ ___

| | | | | | | |

Add or subtract.

479	611	784	620	326	900
+ 382	− 253	+ 105	− 549	+ 194	− 718

Count by 5s.

735 740

Read and solve.

There were 5 more crabs in the water than on the sand. There were 23 crabs in the water. How many crabs were there in all?

_____ crabs

Circle the fewest number of coins needed to buy the shell.

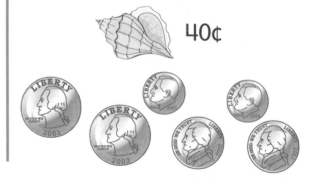

40¢

Write the times. Use **a.m.** and **p.m.**

I eat breakfast.

_____

I eat dinner.

_____

Circle the shapes that can roll.

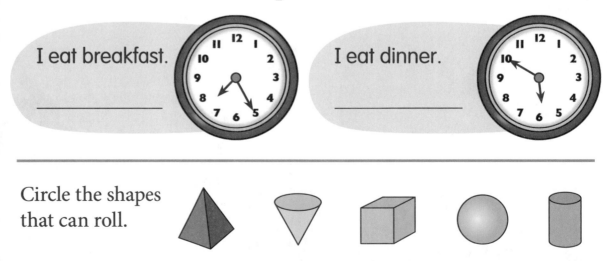

Skill Sharpeners: Math • EMC 8252 • © Evan-Moor Corp.

The Beautiful Sea

Answer Key

Page 6

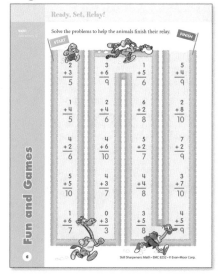

Page 7

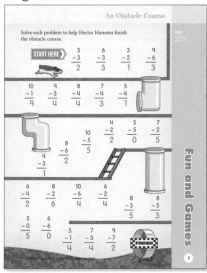

Page 8

Shot Put Contest

Five animals entered the shot put contest. Here are the scores.

Name	First Throw (meters)	Second Throw (meters)
Gogo Gorilla	6	9
Iggy Iguana	6	7
Tuffy Toad	8	9
Millie Moose	5	4
Elmer Elephant	7	8

Add the scores for the first throw and the second throw for each animal. Write the totals in the table.

Name	Total Meters Thrown
Gogo Gorilla	15
Iggy Iguana	13
Tuffy Toad	17
Millie Moose	9
Elmer Elephant	15

Who had the highest total? **Tuffy**
What was the total? **17**
Who had the lowest total? **Millie**
What was the total? **9**
Which two animals had the same total? **Gogo** **Elmer**
What was their total? **15**

Page 9

Page 10

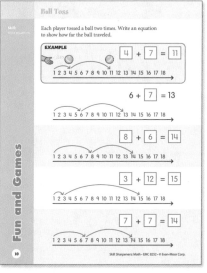

Page 11

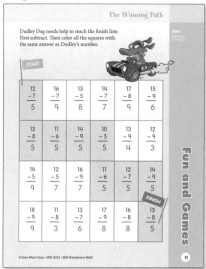

Page 12

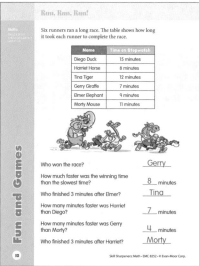

Page 13

Page 14

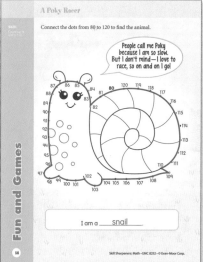

Page 15

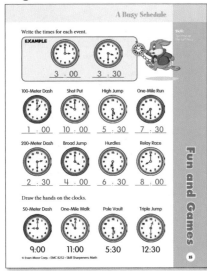

Page 16

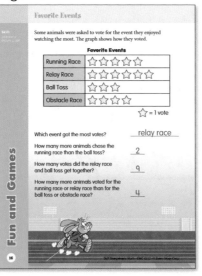

Page 17

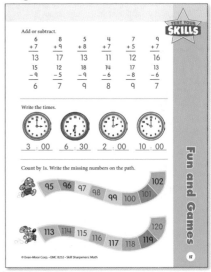

Page 18

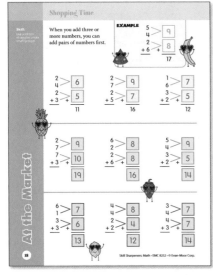

Page 19

Page 20

Page 21

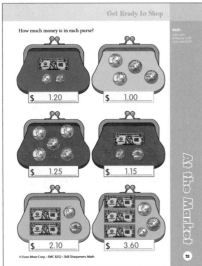

Page 22

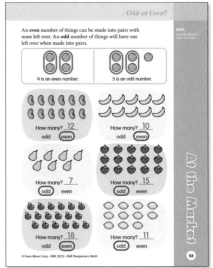

Page 23

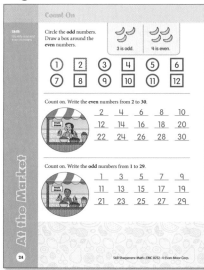

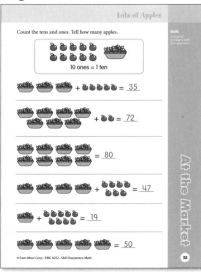

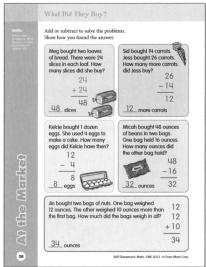

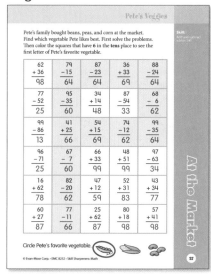

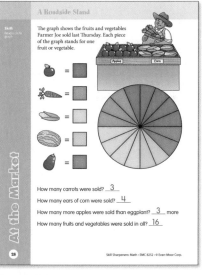

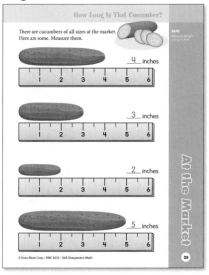

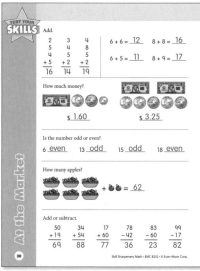

Page 33

A Busy Baker

Look at all the cookies that Andy baked! Circle each row. Count the number of cookies in each row. Then write an addition sentence to show how many cookies Andy made.

$4 + 4 + 4 = 12$

$5 + 5 + 5 = 15$

$3 + 3 + 3 + 3 = 12$

$5 + 5 + 5 + 5 = 20$

How many cookies did Andy bake in all? 59

Page 34

What's in the Kitchen?

Count the number of items in each row. Write an addition sentence to show how many there are.

$3 + 3 = 6$

$4 + 4 = 8$

$4 + 4 + 4 = 12$

$5 + 5 + 5 = 15$

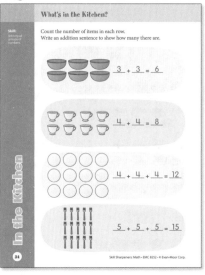

Page 35

Cook Up Some Addition

You can break up numbers to help you add.

EXAMPLE

$$\begin{array}{r} 40 + 5 \\ 20 + 6 \\ \hline 60 + 11 = 71 \end{array}$$

Show how you can break up the numbers to help you add.

$27 + 18 \rightarrow 20 + 7,\; 10 + 8,\; 30 + 15 = 45$

$48 + 36 \rightarrow 40 + 8,\; 30 + 6,\; 70 + 14 = 84$

$39 + 37 \rightarrow 30 + 9,\; 30 + 7,\; 60 + 16 = 76$

$23 + 67 \rightarrow 20 + 3,\; 60 + 7,\; 80 + 10 = 90$

$17 + 76 \rightarrow 10 + 7,\; 70 + 6,\; 80 + 13 = 93$

$38 + 59 \rightarrow 30 + 8,\; 50 + 9,\; 80 + 17 = 97$

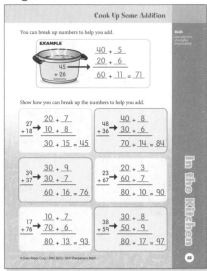

Page 36

Snack Time

Hillary is looking for a snack that has fewer than 200 calories. (A calorie is a unit of measure that tells how much energy your body gets from eating.) Here are some choices. Add to find the number of calories for each choice.

celery and peanut butter
$$\begin{array}{r} 6 \\ + 80 \\ \hline 86 \end{array}$$
86 calories

bread and cheese
$$\begin{array}{r} 100 \\ + 85 \\ \hline 185 \end{array}$$
185 calories

pretzel and peanut butter
$$\begin{array}{r} 108 \\ + 80 \\ \hline 188 \end{array}$$
188 calories

apple and cheese
$$\begin{array}{r} 95 \\ + 85 \\ \hline 180 \end{array}$$
180 calories

6 calories · 95 calories · 80 calories · 108 calories · 100 calories · 85 calories

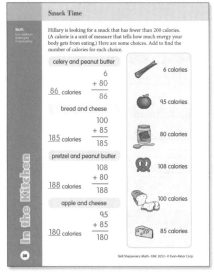

Page 37

Party Food

Solve the problems.

Janna put 21 slices of tomatoes on a plate. Then she added 16 more slices. How many slices of tomatoes were on the plate? 37 slices

Casey bought 2 jars of olives. He put all the olives into a bowl. There were 45 olives in each jar. How many were in the bowl? 90 olives

Kruti made 36 sandwiches. There were 22 turkey sandwiches. The rest had tuna. How many tuna sandwiches were there? 14 sandwiches

Jin made 48 cupcakes. There were 18 with chocolate icing. The rest had vanilla icing. How many cupcakes had vanilla icing? 30 cupcakes

Elina cut one cucumber into 12 slices, another into 13 slices, and another into 15 slices. How many slices did she have in all? 40 slices

There were 64 carrot sticks. After Ryan ate some, there were 51 sticks left. How many carrot sticks did Ryan eat? 13 carrot sticks

Page 38

Add to Check Subtraction

Amira is doing her math homework while she waits for her meatloaf to finish cooking. Help her complete each subtraction problem. Then add to check the answers.

$69 - 23 = 46$ $46 + 23 = 69$ $29 - 16 = 13$ $13 + 16 = 29$ $37 - 24 = 13$ $13 + 24 = 37$

$68 - 45 = 23$ $23 + 45 = 68$ $75 - 34 = 41$ $41 + 34 = 75$ $55 - 35 = 20$ $20 + 35 = 55$

$79 - 35 = 44$ $44 + 35 = 79$ $66 - 32 = 34$ $34 + 32 = 66$ $29 - 26 = 3$ $3 + 26 = 29$

$94 - 53 = 41$ $41 + 53 = 94$ $45 - 30 = 15$ $15 + 30 = 45$ $78 - 43 = 35$ $35 + 43 = 78$

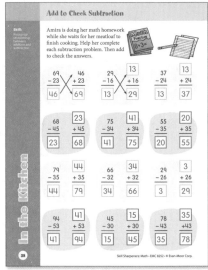

Page 39

Sharing Pizza

You can slice pizza to make equal shares.

two equal shares — This pizza has two **halves**. Each share is called **one half**.

three equal shares — This pizza has three **thirds**. Each share is called **one third**.

four equal shares — This pizza has four **fourths**. Each share is called **one fourth**.

Write what share of pizza has been eaten.

one half · one third · one fourth

Slice the pizza to show equal shares. Draw toppings on the pizza to match the share.

one fourth · one half · one third

Page 40

Family Favorites

Alexa did a survey to see which foods the people in her family liked. She made a table to show the results.

	pizza	hamburger	taco	stir fry	hot dog
Mom	X			X	
Dad	X	X	X		X
Cleo	X	X			
Malcolm	X	X	X	X	X
Alexa	X		X	X	

Use the table to complete this graph.

Family Favorites

Which food did everyone like? pizza

Which food did the least number of people like? hot dog

Which three foods got the same number of votes? hamburger   taco   stir fry

How many votes did each of these foods get? 3

Page 41

TEST YOUR SKILLS

Add or subtract. Fill in the circle to show the answer.

$35 + 24 = 59$ ● 59   ○ 69   ○ 49

$21 + 49 = 70$ ○ 60   ○ 610   ● 70

$67 + 25 = 92$ ○ 82   ● 92   ○ 812

$69 - 36 = 33$ ○ 34   ● 33   ○ 95

$47 - 23 = 24$ ● 24   ○ 80   ○ 69

$64 - 51 = 13$ ○ 18   ○ 15   ● 13

Write an addition sentence to show how many strawberries there are.

$5 + 5 + 5 = 15$

Solve.

Madi made 24 raisin cookies and 18 oatmeal cookies. How many cookies did she make in all? 42 cookies

Draw a line to match.

one third · one half · one fourth

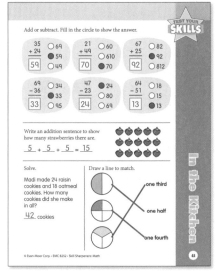

Page 42

Which Ride?

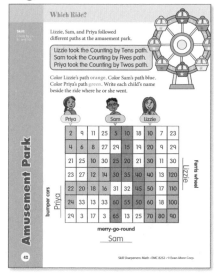

Lizzie, Sam, and Priya followed different paths at the amusement park.

Lizzie took the Counting by Tens path.
Sam took the Counting by Fives path.
Priya took the Counting by Twos path.

Color Lizzie's path orange. Color Sam's path blue. Color Priya's path green. Write each child's name beside the ride where he or she went.

Priya   Sam   Lizzie

2	9	11	25	5	10	18	10	7	23
4	6	8	27	15	19	20	9	29	
21	25	10	30	25	20	30	11	30	
23	27	12	30	35	40	40	13	120	
22	20	16	31	32	45	50	51	110	
24	33	13	30	60	55	60	60	18	100
29	3	17	5	65	13	25	70	80	90

Ferris wheel ___
Lizzie

bumper cars
Priya

merry-go-round
Sam

Amusement Park

Page 43

Cross the River

Carla is playing "Cross the River." She must cross a river full of hungry crocodiles by jumping from rock to rock.

First Carla must solve the problems on the rocks. Those with **even-numbered** answers are rocks she can jump on. Those with **odd-numbered** answers are really crocodiles!

Even numbers end in 0, 2, 4, 6, and 8.
Odd numbers end in 1, 3, 5, 7, and 9.

Help Carla by writing the answers to the problems. Then color the rocks with even answers to make a safe path for her.

$14 - 6 = 8$ $15 - 7 = 8$ $12 - 8 = 4$

$6 + 7 = 13$ $8 + 8 = 16$ $10 - 6 = 4$

$16 - 8 = 8$ $18 - 9 = 9$

$7 + 5 = 12$

$8 + 7 = 15$ $9 + 7 = 16$

$14 - 8 = 6$ $7 + 6 = 13$

Amusement Park

Page 44

Funtime Buys

Theo is in the gift shop at Funtime Park. Here are some items he is thinking of buying. Circle the money he will need.

$5.55 $1.25

$2.35 $4.75

Amusement Park

Page 45

Bull's-Eye!

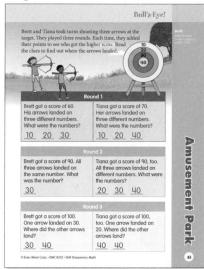

Brett and Tiana took turns shooting three arrows at the target. They played three rounds. Each time, they added their points to see who got the higher score. Read the clues to find out where the arrows landed.

Round 1

Brett got a score of 60. His arrows landed on three different numbers. What were the numbers?
10   20   30

Tiana got a score of 70. Her arrows landed on three different numbers. What were the numbers?
10   20   40

Round 2

Brett got a score of 90. All three arrows landed on the same number. What was the number?
30

Tiana got a score of 90, too. All three arrows landed on different numbers. What were the numbers?
20   30   40

Round 3

Brett got a score of 100. One arrow landed on 30. Where did the other arrows land?
30   40

Tiana got a score of 100, too. One arrow landed on 20. Where did the other arrows land?
40   40

Amusement Park

Page 46

Super-Duper Scoops

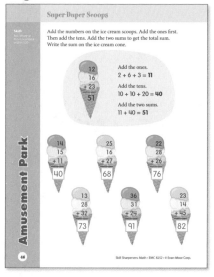

Add the numbers on the ice cream scoops. Add the ones first. Then add the tens. Add the two sums to get the total sum. Write the sum on the ice cream cone.

12
16
+ 23
51

Add the ones.
$2 + 6 + 3 = 11$

Add the tens.
$10 + 10 + 20 = 40$

Add the two sums.
$11 + 40 = 51$

14
15
+ 11
40

25
16
+ 27
68

22
28
+ 26
76

13
28
+ 32
73

36
31
+ 24
91

23
14
+ 45
82

Amusement Park

Page 47

Look at This!

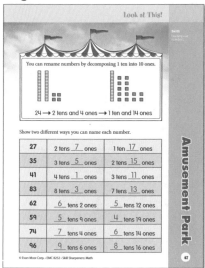

You can rename numbers by decomposing 1 ten into 10 ones.

24 → 2 tens and 4 ones → 1 ten and 14 ones

Show two different ways you can name each number.

27	2 tens 7 ones	1 ten 17 ones
35	3 tens 5 ones	2 tens 15 ones
41	4 tens 1 ones	3 tens 11 ones
83	8 tens 3 ones	7 tens 13 ones
62	6 tens 2 ones	5 tens 12 ones
59	5 tens 9 ones	4 tens 19 ones
74	7 tens 4 ones	6 tens 14 ones
96	9 tens 6 ones	8 tens 16 ones

Amusement Park

Page 48

Tiki's Tickets

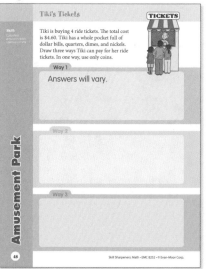

TICKETS

Tiki is buying 4 ride tickets. The total cost is $4.60. Tiki has a whole pocket full of dollar bills, quarters, dimes, and nickels. Draw three ways Tiki can pay for her ride tickets. In one way, use only coins.

Way 1
Answers will vary.

Way 2

Way 3

Amusement Park

Page 49

Pop the Balloons

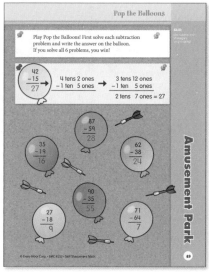

Play Pop the Balloons! First solve each subtraction problem and write the answer on the balloon. If you solve all 6 problems, you win!

42
−15
27

4 tens 2 ones
−1 ten 5 ones
→
3 tens 12 ones
−1 ten 5 ones
2 tens 7 ones = 27

87
−59
28

35
−19
16

62
−38
24

90
−35
55

27
−18
9

71
−64
7

Amusement Park

Page 50

Juggling Jim

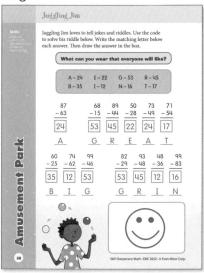

Juggling Jim loves to tell jokes and riddles. Use the code to solve his riddle below. Write the matching letter below each answer. Then draw the answer in the box.

What can you wear that everyone will like?

A – 24	E – 22	G – 53	R – 45
B – 35	I – 12	N – 16	T – 17

87   68   89   50   73   71
−63 −15 −44 −28 −49 −54
24   53   45   22   24   17
A   G   R   E   A   T

60   74   99   82   48   99
−25 −62 −46 −29 −48 −36 −83
35   12   53   53   45   12   16
B   I   G   G   R   I   N

Amusement Park

Roller Coaster Fun

Add or subtract.

40 − 6 = 34	72 + 9 = 81	51 − 5 = 46	32 − 4 = 28
82 − 5 = 77	48 + 5 = 53	65 − 9 = 56	33 − 7 = 26
20 − 3 = 17	90 − 1 = 89	37 + 4 = 41	74 − 8 = 66
50 − 2 = 48	22 − 4 = 18	76 + 7 = 83	63 − 9 = 54
46 − 8 = 38	55 + 9 = 64	89 + 3 = 92	62 + 8 = 70

Amusement Park

Ball Toss

Some children played Ball Toss at the amusement park. Read about how they did. Then solve the problems.

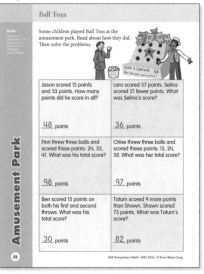

Jason scored 15 points and 33 points. How many points did he score in all?

48 points

Lara scored 57 points. Selina scored 21 fewer points. What was Selina's score?

36 points

Finn threw three balls and scored these points: 24, 33, 41. What was his total score?

98 points

Chloe threw three balls and scored these points: 15, 24, 58. What was her total score?

97 points

Ben scored 15 points on both his first and second throws. What was his total score?

30 points

Tatum scored 9 more points than Shawn. Shawn scored 73 points. What was Tatum's score?

82 points

Amusement Park

Funtime Park's Tick-Tock Shop

When the minute hand is on the 9, it is 45 minutes past the hour.
8:45

When the minute hand is on the 3, it is 15 minutes past the hour.
7:15

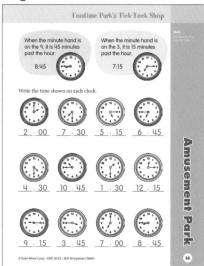

Write the time shown on each clock.

2 : 00   7 : 30   5 : 15   6 : 45

4 : 30   10 : 45   1 : 30   12 : 15

9 : 15   3 : 15   7 : 00   8 : 45

Amusement Park

A Day at Funtime Park

Katie spent a day at Funtime Park. Write the time when she did each activity. Use **a.m.** to show a time before noon. Use **p.m.** to show a time of noon or later.

Katie and her family arrived at the park in the morning. **10:00 a.m.**	She rode the Ferris wheel right after she arrived. **10:30 a.m.**
She went on the roller coaster before lunch. **11:15 a.m.**	Katie and her family had lunch. **12:30 p.m.**
After lunch, she played Ring Toss and won! **1:45 p.m.**	After Ring Toss, she went on a boat ride. **2:30 p.m.**
Katie had ice cream for an afternoon snack. **3:00 p.m.**	Katie and her family went home before dinner. **5:15 p.m.**

Amusement Park

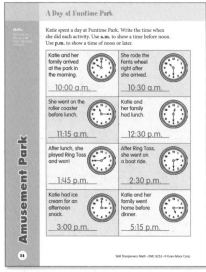

TEST YOUR SKILLS

Add or subtract.

76 − 34 = 42   19 + 52 = 71   80 − 16 = 64

Circle $1.37.   Circle $2.60.

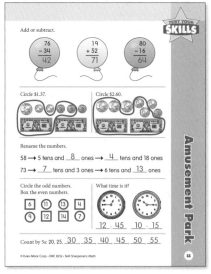

Rename the numbers.

58 → 5 tens and **8** ones → **4** tens and 18 ones

73 → **7** tens and 3 ones → 6 tens and **13** ones

Circle the odd numbers. Box the even numbers.

6   11   13   4
9   12   14   7

What time is it?

12 : 45   10 : 15

Count by 5s: 20, 25, **30**, **35**, **40**, **45**, **50**, **55**

Amusement Park

When Will It Rain?

Add.

16 + 16	1 16 + 16 = 2	1 16 + 16 = 32
Add the ones.	Write the ones. Move the tens to the tens place.	Add the tens.

T	I	A	N	B	F
18 + 8 = 26	33 + 29 = 62	57 + 18 = 75	44 + 28 = 72	65 + 15 = 80	29 + 29 = 58

Y	X	E	O	R	D
15 + 68 = 83	77 + 13 = 90	19 + 47 = 66	38 + 38 = 76	16 + 26 = 42	54 + 19 = 73

Write the letter for each sum to find out when it will rain.

B Y   N E X T
80 83   72 66 90 26

F R I D A Y
58 42 73 75 83

Weather Watch

Rain or Shine

Add.

17 + 7 = 24	15 + 9 = 24	18 + 8 = 26	14 + 9 = 23	19 + 9 = 28
17 + 38 = 55	19 + 15 = 34	19 + 53 = 72	29 + 26 = 55	36 + 19 = 55
28 + 35 = 63	19 + 75 = 94	17 + 24 = 41	39 + 22 = 61	34 + 57 = 91
37 + 19 = 56	33 + 37 = 70	25 + 38 = 63	18 + 37 = 55	42 + 18 = 60

Did you get four answers of 55? If you did, color the sun. If you did not, color the rain.

Weather Watch

How Much Did It Snow?

Subtract.

34 − 6	2 14 3̸4̸ − 6	2 14 3̸4̸ − 6 = 28
Subtract the ones. If you can't, regroup.	Regroup 30 as 20 and 14.	Subtract 6 from 14 and 0 from 2.

53 − 15 = 38	71 − 26 = 45	32 − 24 = 8	58 − 39 = 19
70 − 59 = 11	85 − 38 = 47	94 − 87 = 7	80 − 24 = 56
74 − 59 = 15	46 − 18 = (28)	75 − 57 = 18	50 − 26 = 24

Find out how much it snowed last month. Look at your answers. Circle the number that is greater than 25 but less than 30.

It snowed **28** centimeters.

Weather Watch

Snowman Addition

Add.

45 + 15 + 27 + 32 = 119

31 + 12 + 21 + 63 = 127

12 + 23 + 34 + 45 = 114

26 + 30 + 42 + 10 = 108

61 + 25 + 19 + 35 = 140

52 + 30 + 25 + 47 = 154

45 + 16 + 20 + 24 = 105

North Pole

Weather Watch

Page 60

How Long Are the Snowmen's Noses?

Skill: Measure length using centimeters

These carrots will be used to make noses for four snowmen. How many centimeters long is each one?

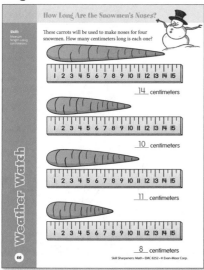

14 centimeters

10 centimeters

11 centimeters

8 centimeters

Weather Watch

60

Skill Sharpeners: Math • EMC 8252 • © Evan-Moor Corp.

Page 61

Snowy Paths

Skill: Count by 2's

Count by 2s. Write the missing numbers on the paths to help the children get home.

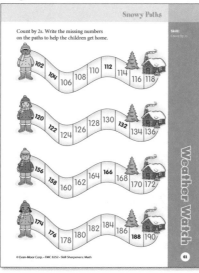

102 104 106 108 110 112 114 116 118

120 122 124 126 128 130 132 134 136

156 158 160 162 164 166 168 170 172

174 176 178 180 182 184 186 188 190

© Evan-Moor Corp. • EMC 8252 • Skill Sharpeners: Math

Weather Watch

61

Page 62

Ready for the Cold

Skill: Count by 5s and 10s

Count by 5s.

105 110 115 120 125

140 145 150 155 160

Count by 10s.

110 120 130 140 150 160

150 160 170 180 190 200

Weather Watch

62

Skill Sharpeners: Math • EMC 8252 • © Evan-Moor Corp.

Page 63

Fun in the Sun

Skill: Recognize relationships between addition and subtraction

Subtract. Then add to check the answers.

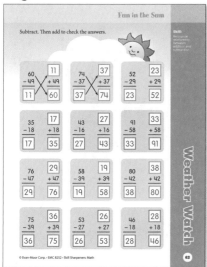

60 −49 = 11	11 +49 = 60	74 −37 = 37	37 +37 = 74	52 −29 = 23	23 +29 = 52
35 −18 = 17	17 +18 = 35	43 −16 = 27	27 +16 = 43	91 −58 = 33	33 +58 = 91
76 −47 = 29	29 +47 = 76	58 −39 = 19	19 +39 = 58	80 −42 = 38	38 +42 = 80
75 −39 = 36	36 +39 = 75	53 −27 = 26	26 +27 = 53	46 −18 = 28	28 +18 = 46

© Evan-Moor Corp. • EMC 8252 • Skill Sharpeners: Math

Weather Watch

63

Page 64

Read the Thermometer

Skill: Read a thermometer

A thermometer measures temperature. It has markings that show how hot or cold it is. Temperature is measured in units called degrees. Each marking on the thermometer stands for 2 degrees.

Read each thermometer and write the temperature.

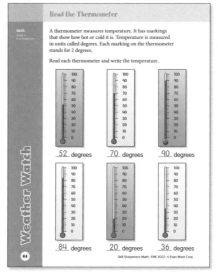

52 degrees   70 degrees   90 degrees

84 degrees   20 degrees   36 degrees

64

Skill Sharpeners: Math • EMC 8252 • © Evan-Moor Corp.

Weather Watch

Page 65

What's the Temperature?

Skills: Solve word problems. Use addition and subtraction strategies beginning

Solve the problems.

The temperature in the morning was 58 degrees. In the afternoon it was 12 degrees higher. What was the afternoon temperature?

70 degrees

It was 54 degrees two hours ago. Now it is 9 degrees warmer. What is the temperature now?

63 degrees

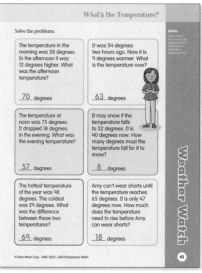

The temperature at noon was 75 degrees. It dropped 18 degrees in the evening. What was the evening temperature?

57 degrees

It may snow if the temperature falls to 32 degrees. It is 40 degrees now. How many degrees must the temperature fall for it to snow?

8 degrees

The hottest temperature of the year was 98 degrees. The coldest was 29 degrees. What was the difference between these two temperatures?

69 degrees

Amy can't wear shorts until the temperature reaches 65 degrees. It is only 47 degrees now. How much does the temperature need to rise before Amy can wear shorts?

18 degrees

© Evan-Moor Corp. • EMC 8252 • Skill Sharpeners: Math

Weather Watch

65

Page 66

Favorite Weather

Skills: Build a bar graph. Add and subtract within 20.

Some students voted for their favorite kind of weather.

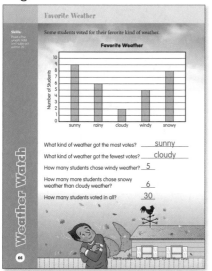

Favorite Weather

What kind of weather got the most votes? **sunny**

What kind of weather got the fewest votes? **cloudy**

How many students chose windy weather? **5**

How many more students chose snowy weather than cloudy weather? **6**

How many students voted in all? **30**

66

Weather Watch

Page 67

SKILLS

Add or subtract. Fill in the circle to show the answer.

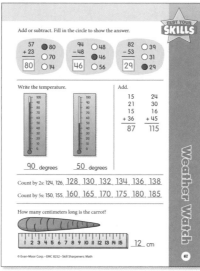

57 +23	● 80 ○ 70 ○ 14
94 −48	○ 48 ● 46 ○ 56
82 −53	○ 39 ○ 31 ● 29

80   46   29

Write the temperature.

90 degrees   50 degrees

Add.

15 21 15 + 36	24 30 16 + 45
87	115

Count by 2s: 124, 126, **128, 130, 132, 134, 136, 138**

Count by 5s: 150, 155, **160, 165, 170, 175, 180, 185**

How many centimeters long is the carrot?

12 cm

© Evan-Moor Corp. • EMC 8252 • Skill Sharpeners: Math

Weather Watch

67

Page 68

Blast Off!

Skill: Count hundreds, tens, and ones.

Count the hundreds, tens, and ones. Write how many blocks there are.

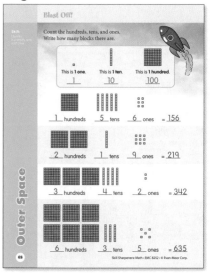

This is **1** one.   This is **1** ten.   This is **1** hundred.

1   10   100

1 hundreds **5** tens **6** ones = **156**

2 hundreds **1** tens **9** ones = **219**

3 hundreds **4** tens **2** ones = **342**

6 hundreds **3** tens **5** ones = **635**

Outer Space

68

Skill Sharpeners: Math • EMC 8252 • © Evan-Moor Corp.

© Evan-Moor Corp. • EMC 8252 • Skill Sharpeners: Math

137

Page 69

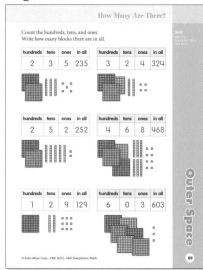

How Many Are There?

Count the hundreds, tens, and ones.
Write how many blocks there are in all.

hundreds	tens	ones	in all
2	3	5	235

hundreds	tens	ones	in all
3	2	4	324

hundreds	tens	ones	in all
2	5	2	252

hundreds	tens	ones	in all
4	6	8	468

hundreds	tens	ones	in all
1	2	9	129

hundreds	tens	ones	in all
6	0	3	603

Page 70

Space Trips

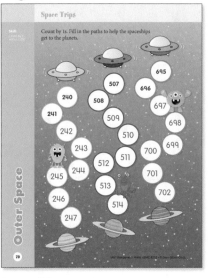

Count by 1s. Fill in the paths to help the spaceships get to the planets.

240, 241, 242, 243, 244, 245, 246, 247
507, 508, 509, 510, 511, 512, 513, 514
695, 696, 697, 698, 699, 700, 701, 702

Page 71

Up, Up, and Away!

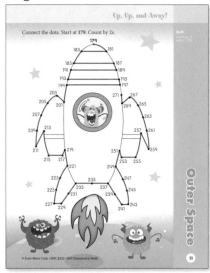

Connect the dots. Start at 179. Count by 2s.

Page 72

Moon Craters

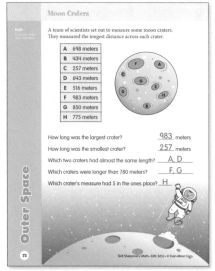

A team of scientists set out to measure some moon craters. They measured the longest distance across each crater.

A	698 meters
B	434 meters
C	257 meters
D	643 meters
E	516 meters
F	983 meters
G	850 meters
H	775 meters

How long was the largest crater? __983__ meters
How long was the smallest crater? __257__ meters
Which two craters had almost the same length? __A D__
Which craters were longer than 780 meters? __F G__
Which crater's measure had 5 in the ones place? __H__

Page 73

A Starry Sky

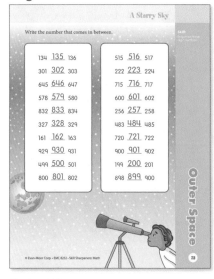

Write the number that comes in between.

134 __135__ 136
301 __302__ 303
645 __646__ 647
578 __579__ 580
832 __833__ 834
327 __328__ 329
161 __162__ 163
929 __930__ 931
499 __500__ 501
800 __801__ 802

515 __516__ 517
222 __223__ 224
715 __716__ 717
600 __601__ 602
256 __257__ 258
483 __484__ 485
720 __721__ 722
900 __901__ 902
199 __200__ 201
898 __899__ 900

Page 74

A Space Robot

Add.

256 +142 = 398	503 +364 = 867	355 +210 = 565
462 +517 = 979	181 +407 = 588	622 +156 = 778
375 +303 = 678	704 +163 = 867	513 +142 = 655

What was the biggest sum? __979__

Page 75

Rodney Rocketeer

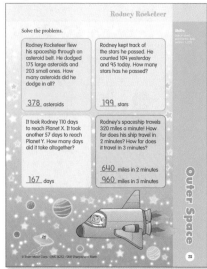

Solve the problems.

Rodney Rocketeer flew his spaceship through an asteroid belt. He dodged 175 large asteroids and 203 small ones. How many asteroids did he dodge in all?
__378__ asteroids

Rodney kept track of the stars he passed. He counted 104 yesterday and 95 today. How many stars has he passed?
__199__ stars

It took Rodney 110 days to reach Planet X. It took another 57 days to reach Planet Y. How many days did it take altogether?
__167__ days

Rodney's spaceship travels 320 miles a minute! How far does his ship travel in 2 minutes? How far does it travel in 3 minutes?
__640__ miles in 2 minutes
__960__ miles in 3 minutes

Page 76

Riddle Time

Use the code to solve the riddle. Write the matching letter below each answer.

If athletes get athlete's foot, what do astronauts get?

E – 139	L – 62	T – 47
G – 278	M – 36	Y – 524
H – 156	O – 89	
I – 41	S – 25	

169 −122 = 47 (T)
386 −230 = 156 (H)
179 −40 = 139 (E)
538 −14 = 524 (Y)
699 −421 = 278 (G)
669 −530 = 139 (E)
757 −710 = 47 (T)

49 −13 = 36 (M)
98 −57 = 41 (I)
87 −62 = 25 (S)
66 −41 = 25 (S)
75 −34 = 41 (I)
89 −27 = 62 (L)
189 −50 = 139 (E)

297 −250 = 47 (T)
899 −810 = 89 (O)
159 −20 = 139 (E)

Page 77

Space News

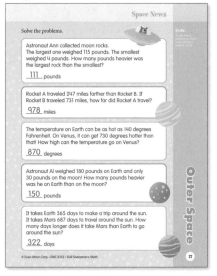

Solve the problems.

Astronaut Ann collected moon rocks. The largest one weighed 115 pounds. The smallest weighed 4 pounds. How many pounds heavier was the largest rock than the smallest?
__111__ pounds

Rocket A traveled 247 miles farther than Rocket B. If Rocket B traveled 731 miles, how far did Rocket A travel?
__978__ miles

The temperature on Earth can be as hot as 140 degrees Fahrenheit. On Venus, it can get 730 degrees hotter than that! How high can the temperature go on Venus?
__870__ degrees

Astronaut Al weighed 180 pounds on Earth and only 30 pounds on the moon! How many pounds heavier was he on Earth than on the moon?
__150__ pounds

It takes Earth 365 days to make a trip around the sun. It takes Mars 687 days to travel around the sun. How many days longer does it take Mars than Earth to go around the sun?
__322__ days

Page 78

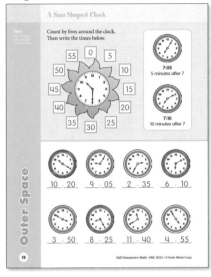

A Sun-Shaped Clock

Count by fives around the clock.
Then write the times below.

55 · 0 · 5
50 · 10
45 · 15
40 · 20
35 · 30 · 25

7:05
5 minutes after 7

7:10
10 minutes after 7

10 : 20   9 : 05   2 : 35   6 : 10

3 : 50   8 : 25   11 : 40   4 : 55

Outer Space

Page 79

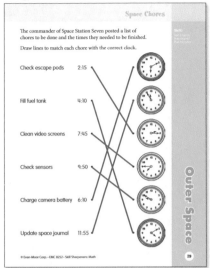

Space Chores

The commander of Space Station Seven posted a list of chores to be done and the times they needed to be finished.

Draw lines to match each chore with the correct clock.

Check escape pods — 2:15

Fill fuel tank — 4:10

Clean video screens — 7:45

Check sensors — 9:50

Charge camera battery — 6:10

Update space journal — 11:55

Outer Space

Page 80

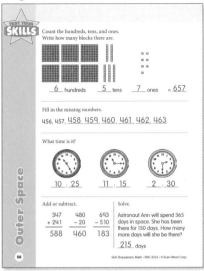

TEST YOUR SKILLS

Count the hundreds, tens, and ones.
Write how many blocks there are.

_6_ hundreds   _5_ tens   _7_ ones = 657

Fill in the missing numbers.

456, 457, _458_, _459_, 460, 461, 462, _463_

What time is it?

10 : 25   11 : 15   2 : 30

Add or subtract.

347	480	693
+ 241	− 20	− 510
588	460	183

Solve.

Astronaut Ann will spend 365 days in space. She has been there for 150 days. How many more days will she be there?

_215_ days

Outer Space

Page 81

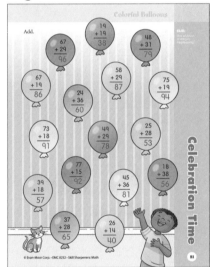

Colorful Balloons

Add.

67 + 29 = 96
19 + 19 = 38
48 + 31 = 79
67 + 19 = 86
58 + 29 = 87
75 + 19 = 94
24 + 36 = 60
73 + 18 = 91
49 + 29 = 78
25 + 28 = 53
77 + 15 = 92
45 + 36 = 81
18 + 38 = 56
39 + 18 = 57
37 + 28 = 65
26 + 14 = 40

Celebration Time

Page 82

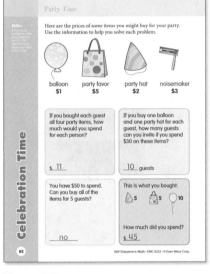

Party Time

Here are the prices of some items you might buy for your party. Use the information to help you solve each problem.

balloon **$1**   party favor **$5**   party hat **$2**   noisemaker **$3**

If you bought each guest all four party items, how much would you spend for each person?

$ _11_

If you buy one balloon and one party hat for each guest, how many guests can you invite if you spend $30 on these items?

_10_ guests

You have $50 to spend. Can you buy all of the items for 5 guests?

_no_

This is what you bought:
5   5   10

How much did you spend?

$ _45_

Celebration Time

Page 83

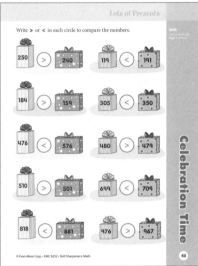

Lots of Presents

Write > or < in each circle to compare the numbers.

250 > 240   119 < 191

184 > 159   305 < 350

476 < 576   480 > 479

510 > 501   699 < 709

818 < 881   976 > 967

Celebration Time

Page 84

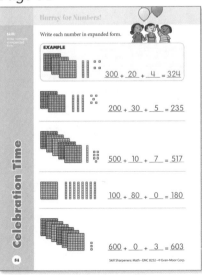

Hurray for Numbers!

Write each number in expanded form.

EXAMPLE

300 + 20 + 4 = 324

200 + 30 + 5 = 235

500 + 10 + 7 = 517

100 + 80 + 0 = 180

600 + 0 + 3 = 603

Celebration Time

Page 85

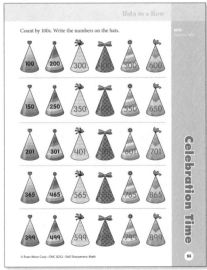

Hats in a Row

Count by 100s. Write the numbers on the hats.

100 200 300 400 500 600

150 250 350 450 550 650

201 301 401 501 601 701

365 465 565 665 765 865

399 499 599 699 799 899

Celebration Time

Page 86

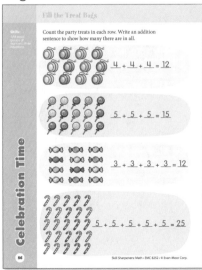

Fill the Treat Bags

Count the party treats in each row. Write an addition sentence to show how many there are in all.

_4_ + _4_ + _4_ = _12_

_5_ + _5_ + _5_ = _15_

_3_ + _3_ + _3_ + _3_ = _12_

_5_ + _5_ + _5_ + _5_ + _5_ = _25_

Celebration Time

Page 87

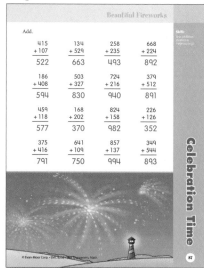

Beautiful Fireworks — Add.

415 +107 = 522	134 +529 = 663	258 +235 = 493	668 +224 = 892
186 +408 = 594	503 +327 = 830	724 +216 = 940	379 +512 = 891
459 +118 = 577	168 +202 = 370	824 +158 = 982	226 +126 = 352
375 +416 = 791	641 +109 = 750	857 +137 = 994	349 +544 = 893

Page 88

Happy New Year! — Add.

256 +362 = 618	381 +139 = 520	582 +225 = 807	446 +371 = 817
755 +153 = 908	742 +191 = 933	371 +385 = 756	590 +148 = 738
762 +165 = 927	483 +372 = 855	559 +360 = 919	133 +482 = 615
183 +286 = 469	476 +260 = 736	214 +193 = 407	562 +154 = 716

Page 89

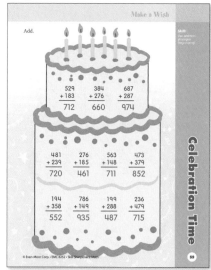

Make a Wish — Add.

529 +183 = 712, 384 +276 = 660, 687 +287 = 974
481 +239 = 720, 276 +185 = 461, 563 +148 = 711, 473 +379 = 852
194 +358 = 552, 786 +149 = 935, 199 +288 = 487, 236 +479 = 715

Page 90

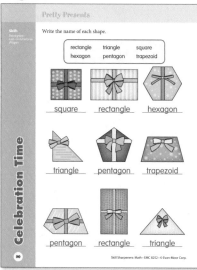

Pretty Presents — Write the name of each shape.

square, rectangle, hexagon
triangle, pentagon, trapezoid
pentagon, rectangle, triangle

Page 91

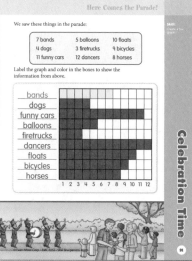

Here Comes the Parade!

Page 92

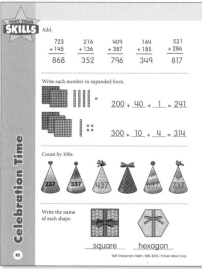

Test Your Skills — Add.

723 +145 = 868, 216 +136 = 352, 409 +387 = 796, 164 +185 = 349, 531 +286 = 817

Write each number in expanded form.
200 + 40 + 1 = 241
300 + 10 + 4 = 314

Count by 100s. 237, 337, 437, 537, 637, 737

Write the name of each shape. square, hexagon

Page 93

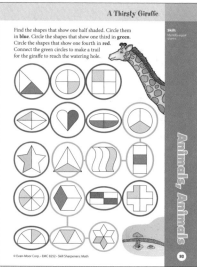

A Thirsty Giraffe

Page 94

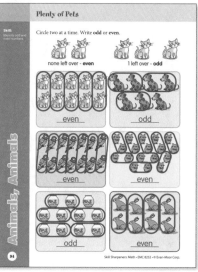

Plenty of Pets — Circle two at a time. Write odd or even.

even, odd
even, even
odd, even

Page 95

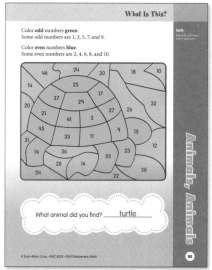

What Is This?

What animal did you find? turtle

Page 96

Heading Home

Help Buzz find his way back to the hive. Start at 96. Count by 10s and connect the flowers that Buzz visits.

Page 97

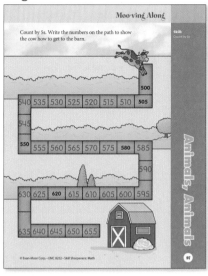

Moo-ving Along

Count by 5s. Write the numbers on the path to show the cow how to get to the barn.

Page 98

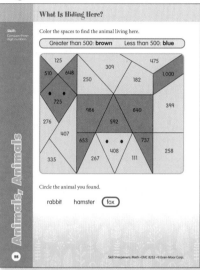

What Is Hiding Here?

Color the spaces to find the animal living here.

Greater than 500: **brown**   Less than 500: **blue**

Circle the animal you found.

rabbit   hamster   (fox)

Page 99

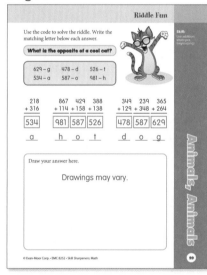

Riddle Fun

Use the code to solve the riddle. Write the matching letter below each answer.

What is the opposite of a cool cat?

629 – g	478 – d
526 – t	534 – a
587 – o	981 – h

218 + 316	867 + 114	429 + 158	388 + 138	349 + 129	239 + 348	365 + 264
534	981	587	526	478	587	629
a	h	o	t	d	o	g

Draw your answer here.

Drawings may vary.

Page 100

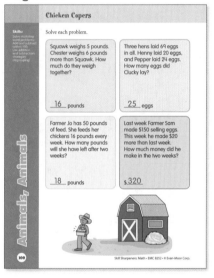

Chicken Capers

Solve each problem.

Squawk weighs 5 pounds. Chester weighs 6 pounds more than Squawk. How much do they weigh together?

___16___ pounds

Three hens laid 69 eggs in all. Henny laid 20 eggs, and Pepper laid 24 eggs. How many eggs did Clucky lay?

___25___ eggs

Farmer Jo has 50 pounds of feed. She feeds her chickens 16 pounds every week. How many pounds will she have left after two weeks?

___18___ pounds

Last week Farmer Sam made $150 selling eggs. This week he made $20 more than last week. How much money did he make in the two weeks?

$___320___

Page 101

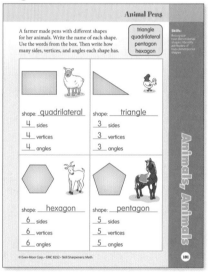

Animal Pens

A farmer made pens with different shapes for her animals. Write the name of each shape. Use the words from the box. Then write how many sides, vertices, and angles each shape has.

triangle
quadrilateral
pentagon
hexagon

shape: _quadrilateral_
4 sides
4 vertices
4 angles

shape: _triangle_
3 sides
3 vertices
3 angles

shape: _hexagon_
6 sides
6 vertices
6 angles

shape: _pentagon_
5 sides
5 vertices
5 angles

Page 102

Sticker Buys

Devon collects stickers of animals. Write how many coins he can use to buy the stickers below. Show the fewest coins each time.

15¢		1	1	
20¢		2		
32¢	1		1	2
28¢	1			3
50¢	2			
43¢	1	1	1	3
65¢	2	1	1	
39¢	1	1		4

Page 103

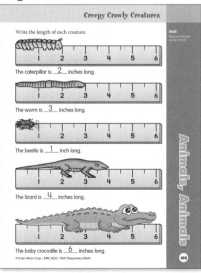

Creepy Crawly Creatures

Write the length of each creature.

The caterpillar is __2__ inches long.

The worm is __3__ inches long.

The beetle is __1__ inch long.

The lizard is __4__ inches long.

The baby crocodile is __6__ inches long.

Page 104

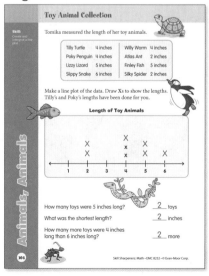

Toy Animal Collection

Tomika measured the length of her toy animals.

Tilly Turtle	4 inches	Willy Worm	4 inches
Poky Penguin	4 inches	Atlas Ant	2 inches
Lizzy Lizard	5 inches	Finley Fish	5 inches
Slippy Snake	6 inches	Silky Spider	2 inches

Make a line plot of the data. Draw Xs to show the lengths. Tilly's and Poky's lengths have been done for you.

Length of Toy Animals

How many toys were 5 inches long? ___2___ toys

What was the shortest length? ___2___ inches

How many more toys were 4 inches long than 6 inches long? ___2___ more

Page 105

Write **half**, **third**, or **fourth** to describe the shaded part.

fourth   half   third

Write the numbers on the correct line.   16   21   29   38   50   73

odd   21, 29, 73   even   16, 38, 50

Add.

401 + 279	364 + 182	151 + 183	208 + 312	627 + 185
680	546	334	520	812

Count by 10s.

178   188   198   208   218   228   238

Name each shape. Write the number of sides, vertices, and angles.

shape: pentagon
5 sides
5 vertices
5 angles

shape: hexagon
6 sides
6 vertices
6 angles

Animals, Animals

Page 106

A Pretty Garden

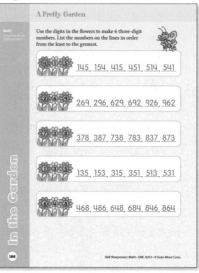

Use the digits in the flowers to make 6 three-digit numbers. List the numbers on the lines in order from the least to the greatest.

4 1 5   145, 154, 415, 451, 514, 541

2 6 9   269, 296, 629, 692, 926, 962

7 3 8   378, 387, 738, 783, 837, 873

1 3 5   135, 153, 315, 351, 513, 531

6 4 8   468, 486, 648, 684, 846, 864

In the Garden

Page 107

Dig into Subtraction

Sometimes you need to regroup to subtract. Solve the problems below. Use the place value blocks to help you.

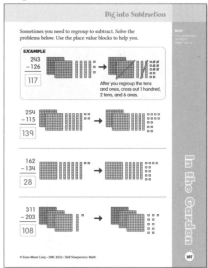

EXAMPLE
243
− 126
117

After you regroup the tens and ones, cross out 1 hundred, 2 tens, and 6 ones.

254
− 115
139

162
− 134
28

311
− 203
108

In the Garden

Page 108

A Garden Riddle

Use the code to solve the riddle. Write the matching letter below each answer.

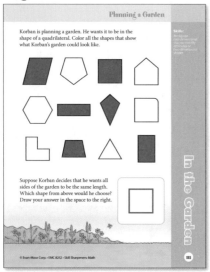

You throw away the outside and cook the inside. Then you eat the outside and throw away the inside. What is it?

354 – A	189 – E	418 – N	247 – R
427 – C	259 – F	571 – O	

492 − 138	757 − 339		293 − 104	581 − 227	675 − 428
354	418		189	354	247
A	N		E	A	R

830 − 259	378 − 119		795 − 368	680 − 109	376 − 129	874 − 456
571	259		427	571	247	418
O	F		C	O	R	N

In the Garden

Page 109

Colorful Blooms

Subtract.

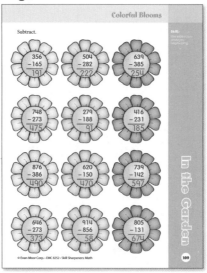

356 − 165 = 191	504 − 282 = 222	639 − 385 = 254
748 − 273 = 475	279 − 188 = 91	416 − 231 = 185
876 − 386 = 490	620 − 150 = 470	739 − 142 = 597
646 − 273 = 373	914 − 856 = 58	805 − 131 = 674

In the Garden

Page 110

Seed Count

Write an equation for each problem. Then solve it.

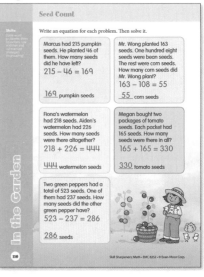

Marcus had 215 pumpkin seeds. He planted 46 of them. How many seeds did he have left?

215 − 46 = 169

169 pumpkin seeds

Mr. Wong planted 163 seeds. One hundred eight seeds were bean seeds. The rest were corn seeds. How many corn seeds did Mr. Wong plant?

163 − 108 = 55

55 corn seeds

Fiona's watermelon had 218 seeds. Aiden's watermelon had 226 seeds. How many seeds were there altogether?

218 + 226 = 444

444 watermelon seeds

Megan bought two packages of tomato seeds. Each packet had 165 seeds. How many seeds were there in all?

165 + 165 = 330

330 tomato seeds

Two green peppers had a total of 523 seeds. One of them had 237 seeds. How many seeds did the other green pepper have?

523 − 237 = 286

286 seeds

In the Garden

Page 111

Planning a Garden

Korban is planning a garden. He wants it to be in the shape of a quadrilateral. Color all the shapes that show what Korban's garden could look like.

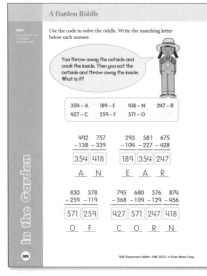

Suppose Korban decides that he wants all sides of the garden to be the same length. Which shape from above would he choose? Draw your answer in the space to the right.

In the Garden

Page 112

What Time Is It?

Write the times.

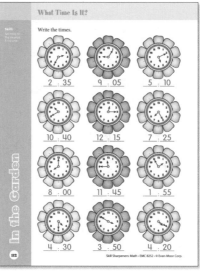

2 : 35   9 : 05   5 : 10

10 : 40   12 : 15   7 : 25

8 : 00   11 : 45   1 : 55

4 : 30   3 : 50   4 : 20

In the Garden

Page 113

Bug Hunt

Teddy went on a bug hunt. The graph shows what he found.

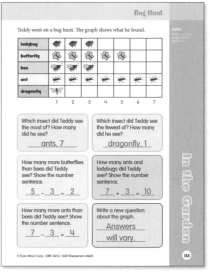

	1	2	3	4	5	6	7
ladybug							
butterfly							
bee							
ant							
dragonfly							

Which insect did Teddy see the most of? How many did he see?

ants, 7

Which insect did Teddy see the fewest of? How many did he see?

dragonfly, 1

How many more butterflies than bees did Teddy see? Show the number sentence.

5 − 3 = 2

How many ants and ladybugs did Teddy see? Show the number sentence.

7 + 3 = 10

How many more ants than bees did Teddy see? Show the number sentence.

7 − 3 = 4

Write a new question about the graph.

Answers will vary.

In the Garden

Page 114

Favorite Flowers

Skill: Read a picture graph

Some children voted for their favorite flower. The graph shows the flowers they chose.

Favorite Flowers

Rose	☺☺☺☺☺
Daisy	☺☺☺☺☺☺☺☺☺
Pansy	☺☺☺☺☺☺
Daffodil	☺☺☺☺☺☺☺

☺ = 1 vote

How many children chose the pansy? __6__

How many children chose the rose? __5__

How many more children chose the daffodil than the rose? __2__

Which flower did the most children choose? __daisy__

How many more votes did the most popular flower get than the least popular flower? __4__

In the Garden

Page 115

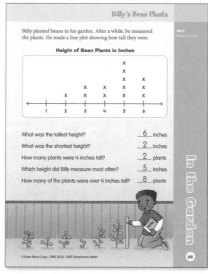

Billy's Bean Plants

Billy planted beans in his garden. After a while, he measured the plants. He made a line plot showing how tall they were.

Height of Bean Plants in Inches

```
                              x
                              x
                    x    x    x    x
          x    x    x    x    x
     1    2    3    4    5    6
```

What was the tallest height? __6__ inches

What was the shortest height? __2__ inches

How many plants were 4 inches tall? __2__ plants

Which height did Billy measure most often? __5__ inches

How many of the plants are over 4 inches tall? __8__ plants

In the Garden

Page 116

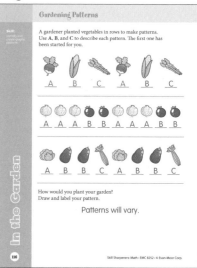

Gardening Patterns

Skill: Identify and create graphic patterns

A gardener planted vegetables in rows to make patterns. Use **A, B,** and **C** to describe each pattern. The first one has been started for you.

A B C A B C

A A B B A A B B

A B B C A B B C

How would you plant your garden? Draw and label your pattern.

Patterns will vary.

In the Garden

Page 117

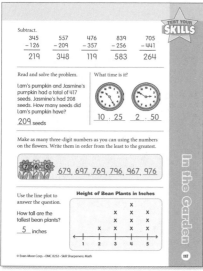

Subtract.

345	557	476	839	705
−126	−209	−357	−256	−441
219	348	119	583	264

Read and solve the problem.

Lam's pumpkin and Jasmine's pumpkin had a total of 417 seeds. Jasmine's had 208 seeds. How many seeds did Lam's pumpkin have?

__209__ seeds

What time is it?

10 : 25   2 : 50

Make as many three-digit numbers as you can using the numbers on the flowers. Write them in order from the least to the greatest.

7 6 9

679, 697, 769, 796, 967, 976

Use the line plot to answer the question.

How tall are the tallest bean plants?

__5__ inches

Height of Bean Plants in Inches

```
               x
          x    x    x
     x    x    x    x
     1    2    3    4    5
```

In the Garden

Page 118

Fishy Facts

Skills: Add and subtract within 20; Add three or more numbers within 20

Add or subtract.

9 +9 = 18	5 +8 = 13	13 −4 = 9	8 +4 = 12	14 −5 = 9	18 −9 = 9
16 −8 = 8	8 +7 = 15	14 −6 = 8	7 +6 = 13	9 +6 = 15	15 −9 = 6
13 −6 = 7	12 −3 = 9	9 +4 = 13	7 +9 = 16	9 +5 = 14	15 −6 = 9
16 −7 = 9	13 −5 = 8	17 −8 = 9	8 +4 = 12	4 +9 = 13	12 −8 = 4
9 5 +1 = 15	8 4 +2 = 14	7 4 +7 = 18	9 4 +0 = 17	4 9 +4 = 17	6 3 +4 = 13

The Beautiful Sea

Page 119

Whale Challenge

Skill: Use addition strategies (regrouping)

Add or subtract.

20 +60 = 80	19 +22 = 41	55 +35 = 90	10 +81 = 91	29 +39 = 68
38 −21 = 17	44 −32 = 12	32 −13 = 19	43 −27 = 16	97 −19 = 78	45 −26 = 19
72 −27 = 45	66 +26 = 92	52 +47 = 99	66 −22 = 44	43 −29 = 14	55 −49 = 6
77 −27 = 50	76 +18 = 94	38 +27 = 65	30 −11 = 19	33 −25 = 8	80 −11 = 69
68 −21 = 47	71 +19 = 90	50 −34 = 16	37 +37 = 74	45 +24 = 69	29 −10 = 19

The Beautiful Sea

Page 120

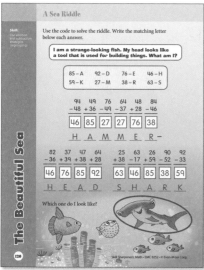

A Sea Riddle

Skill: Use addition and subtraction strategies (regrouping)

Use the code to solve the riddle. Write the matching letter below each answer.

I am a strange-looking fish. My head looks like a tool that is used for building things. What am I?

| 85 – A | 92 – D | 76 – E | 46 – H |
| 59 – K | 27 – M | 38 – R | 63 – S |

| 94 −48 = 46 | 49 +36 = 85 | 76 −49 = 27 | 64 −37 = 27 | 48 +28 = 76 | 84 −46 = 38 |

H A M M E R -

| 82 −36 = 46 | 37 +39 = 76 | 47 +38 = 85 | 64 +28 = 92 | 25 +38 = 63 | 63 −17 = 46 | 26 +59 = 85 | 90 −52 = 38 | 92 −33 = 59 |

H E A D   S H A R K

Which one do I look like?

The Beautiful Sea

Page 121

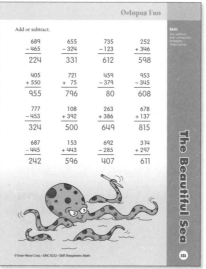

Octopus Fun

Skill: Use addition and subtraction strategies (regrouping)

Add or subtract.

689 −465 = 224	655 −324 = 331	735 −123 = 612	252 +346 = 598
405 +550 = 955	721 + 75 = 796	459 −379 = 80	953 −345 = 608
777 −453 = 324	108 +392 = 500	263 +386 = 649	678 +137 = 815
687 −445 = 242	153 +443 = 596	692 −285 = 407	314 +297 = 611

The Beautiful Sea

Page 122

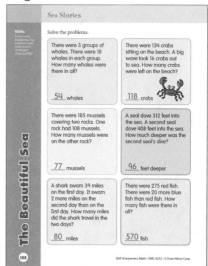

Sea Stories

Skill: Solve word problems; use addition and subtraction strategies (regrouping)

Solve the problems.

There were 3 groups of whales. There were 18 whales in each group. How many whales were there in all?

__54__ whales

There were 134 crabs sitting on the beach. A big wave took 16 crabs out to sea. How many crabs were left on the beach?

__118__ crabs

There were 185 mussels covering two rocks. One rock had 108 mussels. How many mussels were on the other rock?

__77__ mussels

A seal dove 312 feet into the sea. A second seal dove 408 feet into the sea. How much deeper was the second seal's dive?

__96__ feet deeper

A shark swam 39 miles on the first day. It swam 2 more miles on the second day than on the first day. How many miles did the shark travel in the two days?

__80__ miles

There were 275 red fish. There were 20 more blue fish than red fish. How many fish were there in all?

__570__ fish

The Beautiful Sea

Page 123

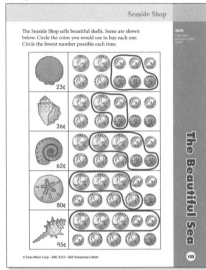

Seaside Shop

The Seaside Shop sells beautiful shells. Some are shown below. Circle the coins you would use to buy each one. Circle the fewest number possible each time.

23¢
36¢
62¢
80¢
95¢

Page 124

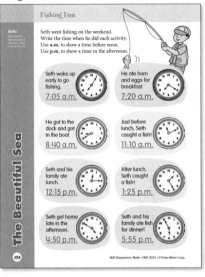

Fishing Fun

Seth went fishing on the weekend. Write the time when he did each activity. Use **a.m.** to show a time before noon. Use **p.m.** to show a time in the afternoon.

Seth woke up early to go fishing.
7:05 a.m.

He ate ham and eggs for breakfast.
7:20 a.m.

He got to the dock and got in the boat.
8:40 a.m.

Just before lunch, Seth caught a fish!
11:10 a.m.

Seth and his family ate lunch.
12:15 p.m.

After lunch, Seth caught a fish!
1:25 p.m.

Seth got home late in the afternoon.
4:50 p.m.

Seth and his family ate fish for dinner!
5:55 p.m.

Page 125

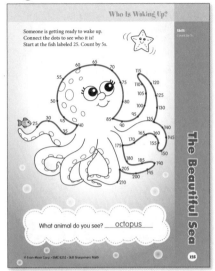

Who Is Waking Up?

Someone is getting ready to wake up. Connect the dots to see who it is! Start at the fish labeled 25. Count by 5s.

What animal do you see? __octopus__

Page 126

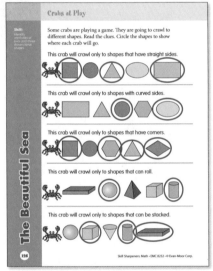

Crabs at Play

Some crabs are playing a game. They are going to crawl to different shapes. Read the clues. Circle the shapes to show where each crab will go.

This crab will crawl only to shapes that have straight sides.

This crab will crawl only to shapes with curved sides.

This crab will crawl only to shapes that have corners.

This crab will crawl only to shapes that can roll.

This crab will crawl only to shapes that can be stacked.

Page 127

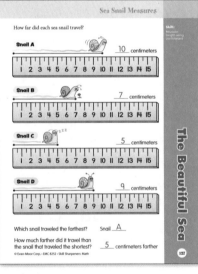

Sea Snail Measures

How far did each sea snail travel?

Snail A __10__ centimeters

Snail B __7__ centimeters

Snail C __5__ centimeters

Snail D __9__ centimeters

Which snail traveled the farthest? Snail __A__

How much farther did it travel than the snail that traveled the shortest? __5__ centimeters farther

Page 128

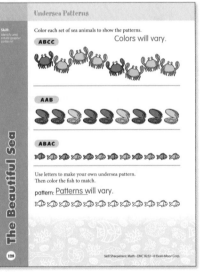

Undersea Patterns

Color each set of sea animals to show the patterns.

ABCC   Colors will vary.

AAB

ABAC

Use letters to make your own undersea pattern. Then color the fish to match.

pattern: __Patterns will vary.__

Page 129

What's the Pattern?

Finish the number patterns. Then write the rule in the boxes.

1 3 5 7 9 11 13 15
+2 +2 +2 +2 +2 +2 +2

15 13 11 9 7 5 3 1
−2 −2 −2 −2 −2 −2 −2

1 6 5 10 9 14 13 18
+5 −1 +5 −1 +5 −1 +5

Page 130

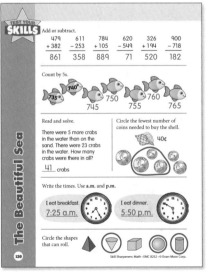

TEST YOUR SKILLS

Add or subtract.

479	611	784	620	326	900
+ 382	− 253	+ 105	− 549	+ 194	− 718
861	358	889	71	520	182

Count by 5s.

735 740 745 750 755 760 765

Read and solve.
There were 5 more crabs in the water than on the sand. There were 23 crabs in the water. How many crabs were there in all?
__41__ crabs

Circle the fewest number of coins needed to buy the shell.
40¢

Write the times. Use **a.m.** and **p.m.**

I eat breakfast.
7:25 a.m.

I eat dinner.
5:50 p.m.

Circle the shapes that can roll.